MW00991795

THE YUPPIE HANDBOOK

THE YUPPIE HANDBOOK

The State-of-the Art Manual for Young Urban Professionals

Marissa Piesman
and Marilee Hartley

Produced by Connie Berman and Roseann Hirsch
Illustrated by Lonni Sue Johnson

LONG SHADOW BOOKS
PUBLISHED BY POCKET BOOKS NEW YORK

Most Long Shadow Books are available at special quantity discounts for bulk purchases for sales promotions, premiums or fund raising. Special books or book excerpts can also be created to fit specific needs.

For details write the office of the Vice President of Special Markets, Pocket Books, 1230 Avenue of the Americas, New York, New York 10020.

Another *Original* publication of LONG SHADOW BOOKS

A Long Shadow Book published by
POCKET BOOKS, a division of Simon & Schuster, Inc.
1230 Avenue of the Americas, New York, N.Y. 10020

Copyright © 1984 by Marissa Piesman, Marilee Hartley
and Ultra Communications, Inc.

All rights reserved, including the right to reproduce
this book or portions thereof in any form whatsoever.
For information address Long Shadow Books, 1230
Avenue of the Americas, New York, N.Y. 10020

ISBN: 0-671-47684-X

First Pocket Books printing January, 1984

Book design by Jacques Chazaud

10 9 8 7 6 5 4 3 2 1

LONG SHADOW BOOKS and colophon are
trademarks of Simon & Schuster, Inc.

Printed in the U.S.A.

ACKNOWLEDGMENTS

To John Bolt, Cheryl Hartley, Twilah and Richard Smith, Jeanette Clafin, Ann Roberts, Dan George, Christine Ash, Gail Collins, Conrad Grove, Jack Easton, Roger Miller, Christian Blake, Jean Crichton, Betsy Haggerty, Marsha Sleeth, Jonathan Weiner, Ed Piehl, Martha and Phil Sullivan, Klaus Winklemann, David Branco, Paul Drolet, Barbara Taylor, Judith Holtzer and the Baltimores, Karen Foss, Mark Aleshnik, Jill Paznik, Sally Rickerman, John Robbins, Tim Showalter, Sam Posner, John Whited, Gary Gleason, Barton Canfield, Patricia Gleason, Mary Salzman, Stephanie Parker, Scott Hummiston.

To Jeffrey Marks, Blanche Piesman, Amy Stephson, Shannon Such, Ann Patty, Robin Binder, Dan Clifton, Esther Cohen, Peter Odabashian, Bruce Kitzmeyer, Sherrill Kurland, Wendy Parmet, Gina Novendstern, Ken Rosenfeld, Vivien Wolsk, Jonathan Beyer, Jean Gallancy, Rhonda Greenstein, Nancy Haber, Joanne Johnson, Diana Lee, Nick Levidy, Kevin McConnell, James Morrissey, Phyllis Ohlandt, Bernard Polak, Kate Quinn, Elaine Reid, Susan Rifkin, Jane Rosenberg, Ollie Rosengart, Barbara Stein, Sonja Talesnik, to Stephen Leon for his help in overcoming technophobia, and to all the other Yuppies in our offices, therapy groups, summer houses and health clubs.

Special thanks to Candy Dato for networking at the Caffe Sha Sha and C. Murphy Archibald of Eufalah, Alabama, and the world for properly introducing the authors. For their help on Yuppies across the country, Andrea Prager, Dorothy Weddell, David Hurlbut, Andy Dash, Mindy Jaffe, Morris Gardner, Melanie Hudak, Cathy Beck, Harold Shumacher, Carol Kealy, Mike Bauer, Sharon Peters, Joe Pollack, Martha Nesbit, Karin Winegar, James Martin, Molly Abraham, Susan Steiger, Ellen and Les Schwab, Freda Pines, Mark Silver, JoEllen Ademski, Dorothee Polson, Dennis Getto, Bob Michelet, Alf Collins, Cynthia Reece, Michael (O.J.) Nelson, Michael Carlton, Lucy Cooper, Sandra Early, James Neff.

To Yuppie Editors Marty Asher and Trish Todd.

To our Yuppie Lawyer, Richard Heller.
To our Yuppie agent, Al Zuckerman.
To Patricia Brennan for her cheerful and never-ending support, enthusiasm, and typing skills.
To Joshua Rubin for kid consulting.
To Sam Rubin, Yuppie Restaurateur.
To J.J.H. for not being a Yuppie.
To Barry Hirsch, who supports my Yuppie habits.
To Brian and Nicky Hirsch for being there.
To Jonathan Hirsch, who waited until this book was almost done to get born.

CONTENTS

THE YUPPIE HANDBOOK

BEYOND THE PREPPIE

1. Yuppie: A Dictionary Definition

Yuppie or Yuppy ('yəp-ē) pl. **Yuppies:** (hot, new name for Young Urban Professional): A person of either sex who meets the following criteria: 1) resides in or near one of the major cities; 2) claims to be between the ages of 25 and 45; 3) lives on aspirations of glory, prestige, recognition, fame, social status, power, money or any and all combinations of the above; 4) anyone who brunches on the weekend or works out after work. The term crosses ethnic, sexual, geographic—even class—boundaries. Adj.: Yuppiesque, Yuppie-like, Yuppish, à la Yuppie. See also *fast trackers, baby boomers*. ■

2. Yuppie: A Case Study

IT'S MIDNIGHT ON the waterfront. The mist casts a halo around the streetlamps as the haunting sound of a foghorn breaks somewhere in the distance. Dilapidated factory buildings line the deserted street. A solitary light shines in a window overlooking the water. Below, a lone figure walks the cobblestoned street. He stops to pull his collar up against the dampness. The pocket of his Burberry trenchcoat bulges mysteriously. He carries a leather case secured by a combination lock and initialed in gold with the letters MM. Tall and powerfully built, his broad shoulders strain against his coat. As he resumes his steps, he checks his watch, a handsome gold Rolex. He shakes his head and mutters to himself.

He reaches the building with the light shining in the window and unfastens an intricate set of locks. As he mounts the stairs, a tall blonde in a diaphanous negligee—her tight muscular body seductively visible beneath—opens the door at the top. She holds out a glass of wine and beckons to him invitingly. A large, bearlike dog stands guard at her side.

"Hard day at the office, dear?" she asks.

"Absolute murder," he replies, as he strides toward a large overstuffed sofa and kicks off his Gucci loafers. "That damn brief still isn't done and four of us are working on it. What time did you get in?"

"About ten. After our squash game, we stopped at that new Mexican restaurant around the corner and then I came straight home. I've been working on my

memo. Michael, I forgot to tell you this morning that there's a condominium board meeting scheduled for Thursday at eight."

"Jennifer, you know I have therapy on Thursday. The whole damn board knows I have therapy on Thursday. Why did they schedule it then?"

"I think they need a decision on that special assessment for a sauna on the roof. You'll have to beg off. By the way, did I tell you that the new people in 4 South have an Akita?"

"That makes five in the building, doesn't it?" He turns to the dog. "Did you hear that, Sony? There's a new kid on the block."

Who are these people? What are they talking about? What are two well-educated, affluent people doing living in an old factory building among decaying piers? Most of all, what is an Akita?

Jennifer DesTuileries Harwood Marx is the daughter of old New Orleans aristocracy. She grew up in the Garden district, graduated from Miss Porter's School in Connecticut and majored in art history at Sophie Newcomb College. During her junior year at the Sorbonne, she grew tired of staring at the works of French Impressionists and decided to switch her major to economics. She spent two years

Like Yuppies everywhere, Michael and Jennifer's most cherished goals are:

1. A salary in six figures
2. Live-in help, preferably with breeding, diction and grammar better than the employers'
3. A "home," to use the modest term, that has been photographed by *Architectural Digest,* or at least is a likely candidate
4. The best tables and instant recognition by the maître d's at the top five restaurants in the city
5. Analysis four to five times a week, to question the value of the above

There are certain things Yuppies will never, ever do. They will never:

Eat or drink anything instant
Cancel an hour of reserved court time
Read a tabloid newspaper
Wear any garment with a "permanent press" label in it
Pay cash

They will also never:

Take an afternoon nap (except on New Year's Day)
Give up
Buy something pedestrian like a three-bedroom house in the suburbs for $300,000, when for $450,000 they can have 2,000 square feet of raw loft space in the most run-down section of town and spend another $100,000 renovating it into a haven of high-tech homesteading.

managing the family pepper sauce business and then went on to get an MBA from the Wharton School of Business. Jennifer is now one of the youngest vice-presidents of a large investment banking firm.

Michael Elliot Marx, on the other hand, is the son of a kosher butcher. Raised in Brooklyn, he commuted on the subway to Stuyvesant High School. While Jennifer was making her debut at the Riverboat Cotillion, he was being Bar Mitzvahed at the Twin Decanters. After four years as a scholarship student at Cornell, he went to Harvard Law School and then straight to Wall Street. He met Jennifer at a gallery opening in Soho, and they were married a year later.

Jennifer and Michael are Young Urban Professionals—you can call them Yuppies. Yuppie life is life on the fast track. For Jennifer and Michael, this means billing sixty hours a week,

There is a certain type of Preppie who has crossed class lines and converted to Yuppiehood by doing the following:

1. Traded in his pink LaCoste shirt and madras pants for a Ralph Lauren pinstripe suit and a Gucci pigskin briefcase
2. Dropped his old prep school nickname. (Charles, not Chip, is a more suitable name for someone who negotiates eight-figure corporate mergers.)
3. Replaced his look of smug complacency with the leaner and hungrier look of his ethnic brethren (Remember, these are tough times; if you're not first, you're last.)

working late nights and weekends at the office, bringing the cordless telephone with them when they walk Sony, and taking business trips to San Francisco with no time to eat at Chez Panisse.

Yuppie culture is responsible for the popularity of the new American cuisine, the elevated status of pasta and the proliferation of raspberry vinegar. For Jennifer and Michael, dining has become a religious ceremony; they worship chèvre and arugula. Their kitchen is better equipped than most restaurants, and Jennifer collects food processor attachments the way she used to collect charms for her bracelet. When they're pressed for time, they frequent the local gourmet take-out store, buying expensive, esoteric versions of chicken salad.

But Jennifer and Michael don't let the chicken salad go to their waists. Jennifer walks to work in her running shoes and tucks her pumps into her leather Fendi carry-all. Her bible is Jane Fonda's Workout videotape. No matter how stuffed Michael's briefcase is, there's always room for a squash racquet. Not since the ancient Greeks has there been a culture so preoccupied with physical fitness, and like the Greeks, Jennifer and Michael's credo is: A Yuppie mind in a

Yuppie body—the necessary ingredients for . . . Yuppie love.

They attack all areas of life with the same deliberate seriousness they display on the squash court. The name of the game is THE BEST—buying it, owning it, using it, eating it, watching it, wearing it, growing it, cooking it, driving it, doing whatever with it. This is why Jennifer and Michael never have enough money. Insisting on the best gives them a reason to get up in the morning and bill another ten hours. Michael and Jennifer know deep in the recesses of their Yuppie minds that on the fast track you've got to run fast to stay in the same place. He who hesitates is lost.

Michael and Jennifer are on the couch, watching their video cassette of *Casablanca*. Michael gets up abruptly and walks over to the closet. "I almost forgot," he says. "I brought a bottle of Dom Perignon for our anniversary." He removes the mysterious bulge from his trenchcoat pocket.

"But it's not our anniversary," says Jennifer, taking two Baccarat champagne flutes from the crystal cabinet.

"Of course it is," Michael replies as he pops the cork. "It's been exactly one year since we closed on our condominium."

"Happy anniversary, darling," Jennifer says, staring into Michael's eyes.

"Here's looking at you, kid," says Michael as they click glasses.

"Arf," says Sony. ■

3. Variations on a Theme: Buppies, Puppies, Guppies, et al

YUPPIES, UNLIKE Preppies, come in all ethnic persuasions and from all rungs of the socioeconomic ladder. Some Yuppie variations are distinct enough to have become subcultures.

BUPPIES (Black Urban Professionals)—Usually walk, talk and look exactly like white Yuppies—except that they don't have to worry about getting a tan. The latter characteristic can be a major asset on rainy summer weekends at the beach house and at the beginning of Caribbean vacations, when everyone else is sickly pale. The significant quantity of time usually consumed getting a respectable tan can be devoted instead to improving the backhand and to shopping. This may explain why Buppies are generally better-dressed and in better physical shape than their white counterparts. Other Buppie traits include:

- Greater familiarity with Reggae music—a major asset when island hopping.
- Preference for custom-made business suits (Buppies never wear ethnic fashions like dashikis).
- Tendency to name their daughters Keesha instead of Rebecca.
- If female, the inclination to wear a second pair of pierced earrings with their diamond studs.
- Carefully articulated and accentless speech. During their years at good private schools and big-name colleges, Buppies make sure all regional or ethnic distinctions in their speech are entirely eradicated. Why do you think so many Buppies get jobs as newscasters?

Prominent Buppies: Bryant Gumbel, Arthur Ashe, Bobby Short, André Watts, Diana Ross, Vanessa Williams.

HUPPIES (Hispanic Urban Professionals)—Think Geraldo Rivera.

GUPPIES (Gay Urban Professionals)—Are really super Yuppies because they were the pioneers of Yuppie culture. Guppies formed the first glorified two-income families and played a major part in the Art Deco revival. They will undoubtedly be riding the crest of the next trend while the rest of Yuppiedom is still clinging to its soon-to-be-outdated Fiestaware.

Perhaps because they are trendsetters, Guppies have maintained a distinct subculture, which develops the concept of lifestyle to its fullest potential. Some distinguishing characteristics of this lifestyle include:

- Ardent infatuation with the Body Beautiful. (The socially successful Guppie must have not only the right address, the right career and the right annual income, but also the right pectoral muscles.)
- Summer holidays on Fire Island instead of in the Hamptons.
- Use of free weights instead of Nautilus equipment.
- A highly diverse social life. (A Guppie couple might start the night out at the opera, move on to a *nouvelle* restaurant and end up at a leather bar—shedding layers of clothing as they go.
- Preference for spiffier-than-Brooks-Brothers Italian-cut suits and ventless suit jackets.
- Unless stranded in upstate Alaska, acquaintanceship—if not friendship—with at least one celebrity from the stage, screen, music or art world.

JUPPIES (Japanese Urban Professionals)—Juppies, along with Guppies, have made major contributions to Yuppie culture.

- They have a flair for design, both interior and fashion.
- They have mastered the art of simple but elegant floral arrangements, which are becoming increasingly important in the Yuppie household.
- They usually know someone who can send them an electronic component not yet available in the United States.
- They know what to do with raw tuna.

Prominent Juppies: Kenzo, Seiji Ozawa, Issey Miyake.

PUPPIES (Pregnant Urban Professionals)—Manufacturers of executive maternity clothing have made Puppies nearly indistinguishable from the average female Yuppie—up to a point. Puppies may or may not flaunt their condition, depending on whether or not a promotion is imminent. A common Puppie dilemma is the tough choice between delaying the announcement until the fifth month, thereby taking the chance people will think you've O.D.'d on *nouvelle cuisine,* or making it earlier and possibly losing the promotion. Telltale signs of impending Puppiehood include frequent trips to the bathroom and a box of rice crackers stashed in the desk drawer. ■

4. Yuppie Role Models

HERE ARE SOME superstar self-promoters, who may provide inspiration on the way to the top. Remember, however, that the ultimate goal of a true Yuppie is to be his own role model.

1. **Woody Allen** (Yuppie patron saint)
2. **Bill Bradley** (classic case of Preppie turned Yuppie—may be the first Yuppie President)
3. **Mary Cunningham** (a good Yuppie knows how to recoup her losses)
4. **Nora Ephron** (wrote a novel with recipes—très Yup)
5. **Jane Fonda** (pecs even a Guppie would envy)
6. **Terence Conran** (Yuppies cut their teeth in his store)
7. **Ralph Lauren** (né Lifshitz; you've gotta know when to change your name)
8. **Jane Brody** (Yuppie nutrition guru)
9. **George Lucas, Steven Spielberg, Francis Ford Coppola** (high priests of Yuppie pop culture)
10. **Frank Perdue** (masterminded the designer chicken) ■

5. Some Essential Vocabulary Words

IT IS ABSOLUTELY imperative that you develop familiarity with the following terms. You must be able to use them with a casual fluency that belies the hours you've spent learning what they mean. Don't be intimidated: Remember, a few short years ago you were stumbling over terms like "fettucini Alfredo" and "cash machine."

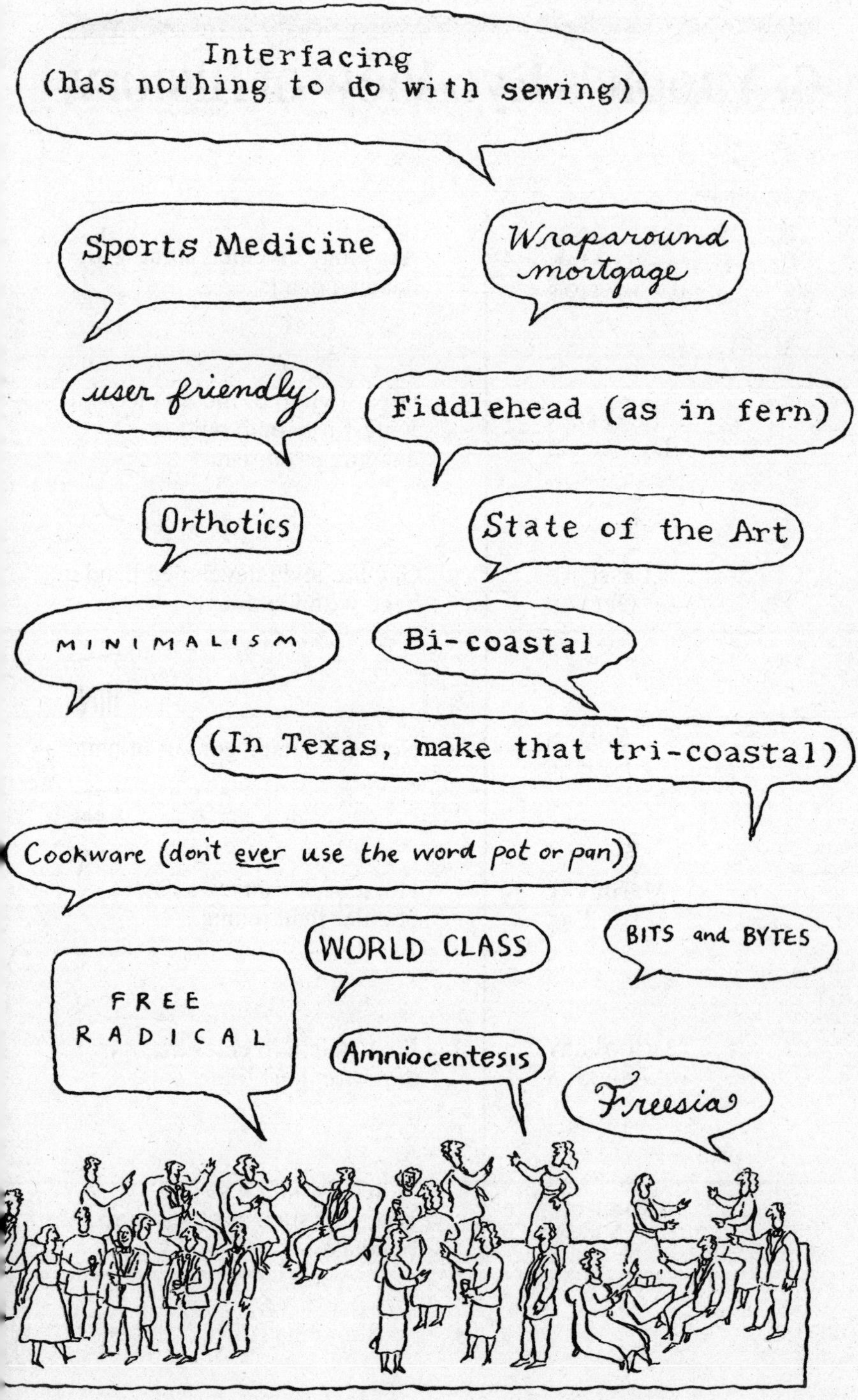
Interfacing (has nothing to do with sewing)
Sports Medicine
Wraparound mortgage
user friendly
Fiddlehead (as in fern)
Orthotics
State of the Art
MINIMALISM
Bi-coastal
(In Texas, make that tri-coastal)
Cookware (don't ever use the word pot or pan)
WORLD CLASS
BITS and BYTES
FREE RADICAL
Amniocentesis
Freesia

6. Yuppie's Eye-View of History

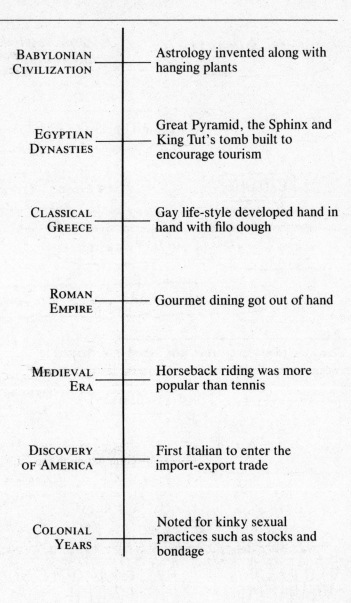

BABYLONIAN CIVILIZATION	Astrology invented along with hanging plants
EGYPTIAN DYNASTIES	Great Pyramid, the Sphinx and King Tut's tomb built to encourage tourism
CLASSICAL GREECE	Gay life-style developed hand in hand with filo dough
ROMAN EMPIRE	Gourmet dining got out of hand
MEDIEVAL ERA	Horseback riding was more popular than tennis
DISCOVERY OF AMERICA	First Italian to enter the import-export trade
COLONIAL YEARS	Noted for kinky sexual practices such as stocks and bondage

EIGHTEENTH-CENTURY BAROQUE PERIOD	Birth of the perfect dinner music
CIVIL WAR	Yankees discover barbecue and mint juleps
WORLD WAR I	Advent of Art Deco followed, along with popularity of leather aviator jackets and Cartier tank watches
GREAT DEPRESSION	Neither Valium nor aerobics had been invented yet
WORLD WAR II	By his frequent trips to Campobello, FDR establishes the second-home market
THE FIFTIES	The McCarthy hearings make lawyers media superstars
VIETNAM WAR	Beginning of VD epidemic culminating in the return of celibacy

7. Your Yuppie I. Q.

IF YOU'RE A BIT insecure about your status as a Yuppie, you can test your Yuppiness by taking the following true/false quiz:

1. Squash racquets have longer handles than those used in racquet ball ☐ True ☐ False
2. A condominium has a Board of Managers, and a cooperative has a Board of Directors ☐ True ☐ False
3, Arugula is a darker green than iceberg ☐ True ☐ False
4. A VHS cassette will not fit into a Betamax ☐ True ☐ False
5. Akitas originated in Japan as temple guard dogs ☐ True ☐ False
6. Starting salaries at some Wall Street law firms have now hit $50,000 ☐ True ☐ False
7. Cross-country skis are narrower than downhill skis ☐ True ☐ False
8. Olive oil should not be stored in the refrigerator ☐ True ☐ False
9. Remote control on a telephone answering machine can be used from anywhere in the world ☐ True ☐ False
10. The term "Jamaican" refers to the origin of a pound of coffee beans, not an ounce of marijuana ☐ True ☐ False

All of the above statements are true. If you thought any were false, study the following chapters carefully. They will help you gain a working knowledge of Yuppie culture, up your Yuppie quotient, and prevent you from falling off the fast track. ■

LIFE-STYLE

8. Y. U. P. I.

Y. U. P. I.

New and Noteworthy

Now available: an electric water softener and PH adjuster made specifically for your relaxation tank. Similar to the ones sold for use on more conventional faucets, this model features a dial with raised digits so that it can be used in the dark.

- A new line of cookware called The Perfect Poacher offers pans designed to fit strangely shaped food. Choose from traditional models, such as salmon and egg poachers, or the more esoteric versions for flounder or eel.
- Now you can take your food processor camping. The first battery-operated machine has just been introduced in the United States; it was test-marketed in France, where it became popular for making ceviche right on the beach and puréeing fresh vegetables without ever removing them from the garden. ■

On the Town: An Eventful Urban Guide

Mini-Marathon: Among the events scheduled this weekend is the third annual Pregnant Women's Marathon, sponsored by Great Expectations, the maternity boutique. This 10-kilometer (6.2-mile) race will begin at 10:30 A.M. at City Hall and will end at Great Expectations, where a high-protein celebration feast will be served to the runners and their parenting partners. The menu will feature tofu ragout with brewer's yeast.

Photography Exhibit: A still life of a wok, a meat cleaver and a ginger root are highlights of a photography show at the Upscale Uptown Gallery. The show features the "Studies in Ethnic Cuisine" series by David Wood, a young English chef-turned-photographer. The exhibit will be on view through the end of next month and includes works entitled "Couscousier and Couscous," "Paella Pan with Saffron" and "Tortilla Press with Cornmeal." ■

Y.U.P.I.

Subway Converted to Housing

An underground subway station has been converted into duplex cooperative apartments with periscopic views of the sidewalks. Prices range from $250,000 for a studio to $700,000 for a convertible two-bedroom. The complex also features health club facilities, running machines on every floor and a restaurant called L'Express Stop.

The complex is divided into four sections, each with a distinctive design theme—Art Deco, Victorian, high-tech and an eclectic decorating scheme entitled "metrograde," which incorporates free-standing graffiti.

The designer, Ralph Mezzo, is a former transit policeman. During the subway strike last year, Mezzo enrolled in the Parker Architectural School and decided to switch careers. ■

Y.U.P.I.

Relationships

Dealing with Your Cleaning Person

A successful relationship with your cleaning person may be very difficult to achieve, according to Constance Heller, author of the recently released book *Coming Clean: An Honest Examination of You and Your Household Help*. Ms. Heller interviewed over a hundred cleaner-cleanee pairs for the book and found that very few had what she considered a healthy relationship.

"There are so many problem areas inherent in the relationship," states Ms. Heller, "that it's rare to find people who can communicate freely and without resentment. You've got to negotiate such sticky issues as how elaborately meals should be prepared, schedule flexibility, how big a Christmas gift to give and how to anticipate cleaning supply needs. In years past, the most common problems were cleaning women who hit the booze or stole the silver. These days you're more likely to encounter the young cleaning man who rummages through your lingerie or plays your erotic films on the VCR. These are tough issues to deal with in a thoughtful and sensitive manner."

The author, a clinical psychologist, has had a steady procession of different cleaning persons through her house, but never thought about the issue until one of her patients asked if she could bring her cleaning lady in for a few joint sessions. The topics discussed during those sessions so intrigued Ms. Heller that she launched a thorough investigation resulting in the publication of her book. ■

Miss Harwood and Lawyer Wed in New York

Jennifer DesTuileries Harwood, daughter of Mr. and Mrs. John Harwood of New Orleans, was married yesterday to Michael Elliot Marx, son of Mrs. Sylvia Marx of Miami Beach and the late Sydney Marx of Brooklyn, New York. Rabbi Shlomo Katz and the Reverend William Worthington performed the ceremony at the Ethical Culture Society in New York.

The bride, an assistant vice-president of Salomon Brothers, a New York banking firm, graduated from Miss Porter's School in Connecticut, Sophie Newcomb College and the Wharton School of Business. She is the granddaughter of Mr. and Mrs. Henry DesTuileries of New Orleans. Mr. DesTuileries is the chairman and president of the Blazin' Cajun Pepper Sauce Company. The bride's father is a professor of cardiology at the Tulane University School of Medicine.

The groom is an associate with the New York law firm of Cadwalader, Wickersham and Taft. He graduated *summa cum laude* from Cornell University and is an alumnus of the Harvard University School of Law. His father was the owner of Très Bon Kosher Meats, a retail meat outlet. The bridegroom's mother is the national vice-president of Hadassah. ■

Y. U. P. I.

FASHION

Henderson's New Line Features Clothing for the Divorced

Jonathan McCall Henderson's fall line for women, unveiled last week, surprised and intrigued the audience of customers and store buyers who packed the showroom. The theme of this innovative collection is "Clothing for the Divorced" and it breaks new ground in fashion history.

Henderson has designed outfits to match the mood of the divorcée as she progresses along the road to emotional recovery. The first grouping, meant for those who are still nursing fresh wounds, is limited to conservative styles in somber greige. "The recent divorcée often just wants to fade into the woodwork," said Henderson. "This boxy wool flannel suit, for example, is the perfect way to do just that." In the next stage, dramatically cut separates in contrasting vivids are designed to call attention to the wearer who is just returning to the social scene. Necklines plunge (albeit discreetly) and hemlines creep ever so slightly upward. The third and final grouping is somewhere between the first two, signaling a return to normalcy. Henderson claims that this group makes the statement, "I'm back to normal; sex is no longer a priority."

The show ended with a bridal gown for the second time around; it is done in creige, a new color developed by Henderson—a combination of cream and beige. "It's an alternative to the traditional and over-used off-white," comments the designer. "The color makes the fashion statement that the wearer has totally integrated her life." ■

Y.U.P.I.

Restaurant Review by LODWICK SWALLOW

Minimal American

☆ ☆ ☆ ☆

The Native Minimalist, a popular new eatery in the fashionable Riverfront Renewal District, specializes in native American cuisine. More important, the skillful management here shows a total understanding of the meaning of dainty portions. There are no unsightly mounds of vegetables or heaping masses of pasta to detract from the visual aesthetic. Here, there is an appreciation for one perfect asparagus spear or one sliver of tender veal, served simply and handsomely.

Our meal began with a superb frog leg marinated in fresh coriander and chili salsa. My friend's stuffed mushroom was slightly overcooked, but gracefully adorned with three fresh American caviar eggs. For the entree, I chose mesquite-grilled squab karaage (made from the delicate third joint of the wing) which was attractively garnished with fresh day lily pistil and stamens. My friend chose a celestial pupik (also known as the Pope's nose) paprikash, made from the tenderest part of the chicken and served with a dumpling. His side dish of five peas completed the color scheme, making the dish lovely to look at as well as to eat. Even the bread stick was fresh, delicious and artfully served with a slender curl of butter.

For dessert, my friend tried the wild grape poached in domestic champagne—a taste delight. My cherry Jubilee flambéed with domestic brandy, alas, was overwhelmed by a teaspoon of freshly made vanilla-bean ice cream. Service was friendly and decidedly understated, and the establishment's excellent selection of domestic wines are always served in tiny sake cups.

The proprietor, Giovanni Radicchio, is a recent convert to New American cuisine. The former owner of Mama Giovanni's Italian Kitchen discovered *nuova cocina* while visiting relatives in Milan. Dining on the light sauces and al dente vegetables there helped him whittle down his 300-pound girth. Back in the United States and weighing in at 150 pounds, he stripped Mama Giovanni's of its plastic grapes and chianti bottles, redecorated the restaurant in its current high-tech style and introduced New American cooking. He also purged his kitchen of all imported ingredients—even Italian olive oil.

The happy result has been that everything, but everything, served at the Native is from domestic sources. Says a deservedly proud Mr. Radicchio: "The wines are from California, the cheese is from Wisconsin and even the seltzer is made in Brooklyn." ■

9. Yupification

THE YUPIFICATION of a neighborhood has been compared to termite infestation. Yuppies descend in swarms and leave nothing behind but dumpsters filled with discarded linoleum. Sure signs of impending Yupification include:

- forced relocation of candy stores and laundromats
- proliferation of gourmet food stores, outdoor cafes, and historical society plaques
- disoriented bums trying to figure out why their favorite bar now has asparagus ferns in the window

Residences are no longer referred to as houses or apartments; they are now called "living spaces." The term is necessarily vague. Factories and garages are being converted into living spaces. Apartments are being converted into two apartments (what once was a foyer is now considered a decent-sized studio). Co-op and condominium conversion is rampant. (Many a bag lady has had nightmares about returning to her train station locker and finding an offering prospectus.) Here is a not unlikely urban scenario:

Struggling immigrant opens a tailor shop in the local ghetto. By working 18-hour days and eating nothing but rye bread, he manages to save enough to open a small dress factory. He rents a floor in a cast iron building and hires a few employees. He marries one of his stitchers, moves to a better neighborhood and sends both his children to city colleges. His son, the accountant, marries a schoolteacher, buys a house with a two-car garage and an acre of wooded property, and sends both of his children to private colleges. The son of the accountant, an investment banker, marries another investment banker and buys Grandpa's dress factory, which has been converted to a "loft living space" and is going for a quarter of a million.

Moral of the Story: Yuppies will live anywhere, as long as the floors are genuine parquet and there's another Yuppie on the block. ■

10. Yuppie Homestyle

THE YUPPIE domicile is part and parcel of everything else in the Yuppie's up-to-the-minute, space-age way of life. While Yuppies usually hire an interior decorator, they must know the basics.

The following general rules apply, whether a renovated Victorian townhouse or a converted industrial loft is being furnished.

Think minimalist. In Yuppiedom, comfort takes a backseat to style. For example, if the living room sofa encourages Saturday mornings plopped in front of the TV instead of jogging around the park, the Salvation Army should be immediately called in to remove the offending piece and a shopping expedition organized to buy either a stiff-backed Breuer chair or a Wassily chaise longue. Either of these can get a wayward Yuppie back on the track.

Plastic Is Poison: Most Yuppies know enough not to have plastic ashtrays around that say "Harvey's Lounge," but there could still be lots of offending little items lurking in unsuspected places. True Yuppies conduct monthly plastic searches, usually starting in the kitchen. Are spice racks, paper towel holders and soap dishes made of wood, wicker or some other appropriate natural material?

In the bathroom, is ceramic or high-tech chrome being used for toothbrush holders and is a real sea shell being pressed into service as a perfect nesting place for the floral English soap? Is the toilet seat oak or maple, or insidious plastic? (Remember: The only place where plastic is not declassé is on the ubiquitous Yuppie push-button phone.)

Other areas to consider in your Yuppie decorating scheme:

Art. An obvious gauge of taste, Yuppies choose carefully and use sparingly. Unblemished expanses of exposed brick can go a long way in the Yuppie decor, but sooner or later you'll have to expose your judgment in paintings, photographs, prints or wall hangings. Unless you really CAN paint, stick to prints or photographs blown up to giant proportions. And don't neglect such rooms as the kitchen and bathroom. This is a test of the truly conscientious Yuppie. Photographs of vegetables are good for the kitchen, and miniatures are okay in the bath.

Antiques. Stay away from anything approaching the Louis XIV era. Really fine Chinese pieces from any era are stylish. And if you're furnishing a restored house built around the turn of the century, some period pieces might be appropriate—especially if it's your country house. Antique farm tools mounted over the hearth go well with a view of rolling hills dotted by silos. City or country, don't be afraid to mix antiques with modern pieces. Anything sold in a modern art museum goes with everything.

Floors. If you're interested in something a bit more daring than parquet, try pickling your parquet and tossing some pastel Dhurrie rugs around to break the monotony of the wood. If the upkeep of pickled parquet gets you down, stick with wall-to-wall industrial carpeting. Floors painted to look like marble are also catching on. Avoid linoleum, little hooked scatter rugs made by your Aunt Bunny in Hackensack, anything they sell at Bargainland or Carpet Universe, and whatever you may have seen in a dentist's office.

Lighting. Buy it in an art supply store or try low-voltage, high-tech floor lamps. Table lamps are out unless they clamp on and bend in half. Track lighting is getting stale.

Walls. Think paint, or possibly lacquer. Light colors—i.e., white or grey—are required. No paper unless it's an authentic pre-Revolutionary design for your authentic pre-Revolutionary country house.

Here are some room-by-room specifics:

Living room—This is the first and possibly only room a guest will see, and the most likely to attract the attention of your local newspaper's style editor. Therefore, it's worth all the attention you can bring to designing this space. You'll want to give the decorator some basic pointers. In furniture, modular sofas are stylish and resilient if you have young children. But Art Deco tables and chests can be quite hardy if well-lacquered. By all means let your furniture float. Avoid right angles and the "place for everything and everything in its place" look. That's perfect for your closet, but if your living room looks the same, people will suspect you of saving cents-off coupons. One wall should be reserved for the obligatory bookcase/desk unit with space for stereo equipment. That

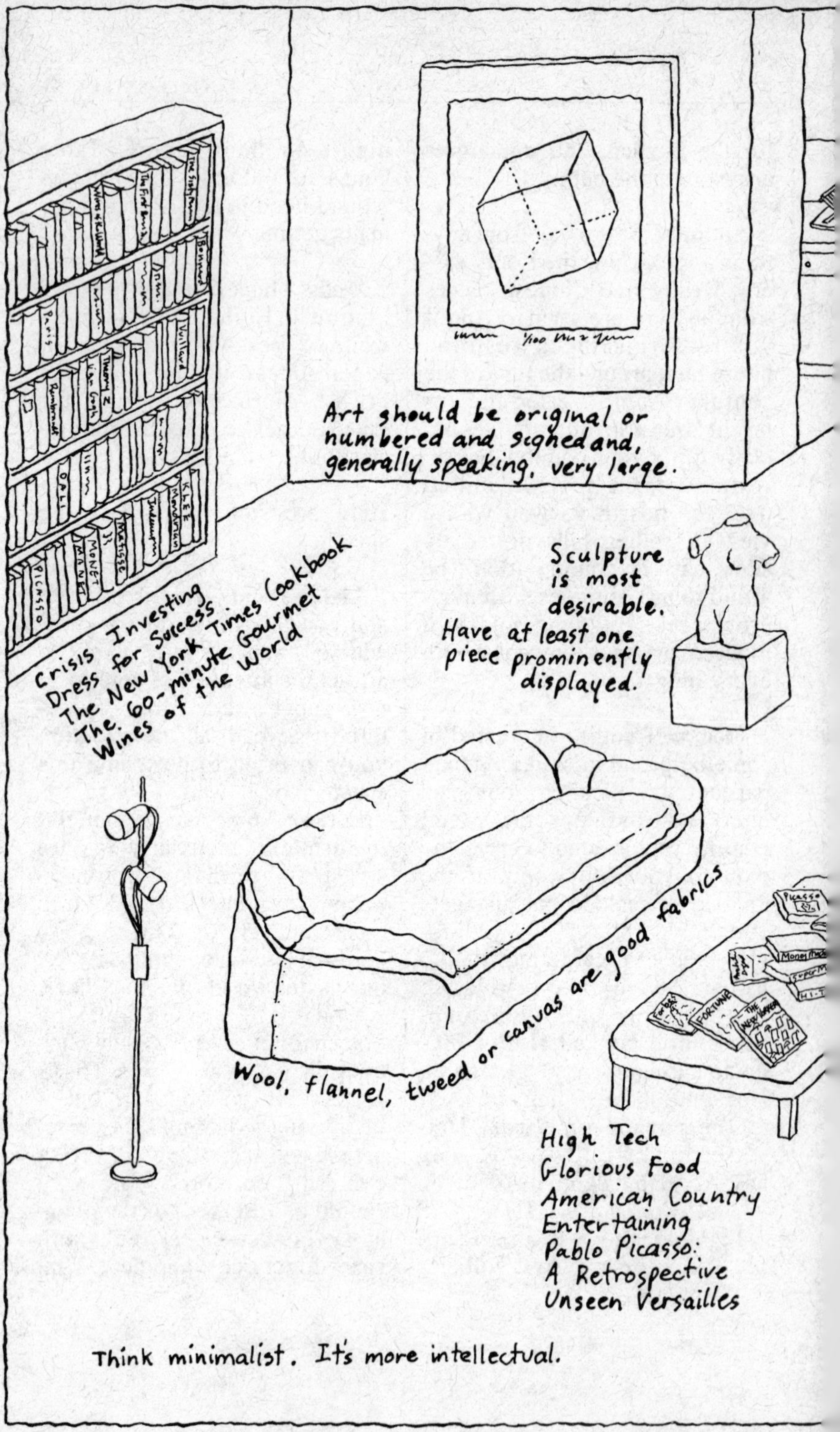

Art should be original or numbered and signed and, generally speaking, very large.
PICASSO
MONET
MANET
MATISSE
KLEE
DALI
Paris
Crisis Investing
Dress for Success
The New York Times Cookbook
The 60-minute Gourmet
Wines of the World
Sculpture is most desirable.
Have at least one piece prominently displayed.
Wool, flannel, tweed or canvas are good fabrics
FORTUNE
High Tech
Glorious Food
American Country
Entertaining
Pablo Picasso: A Retrospective
Unseen Versailles
Think minimalist. It's more intellectual.

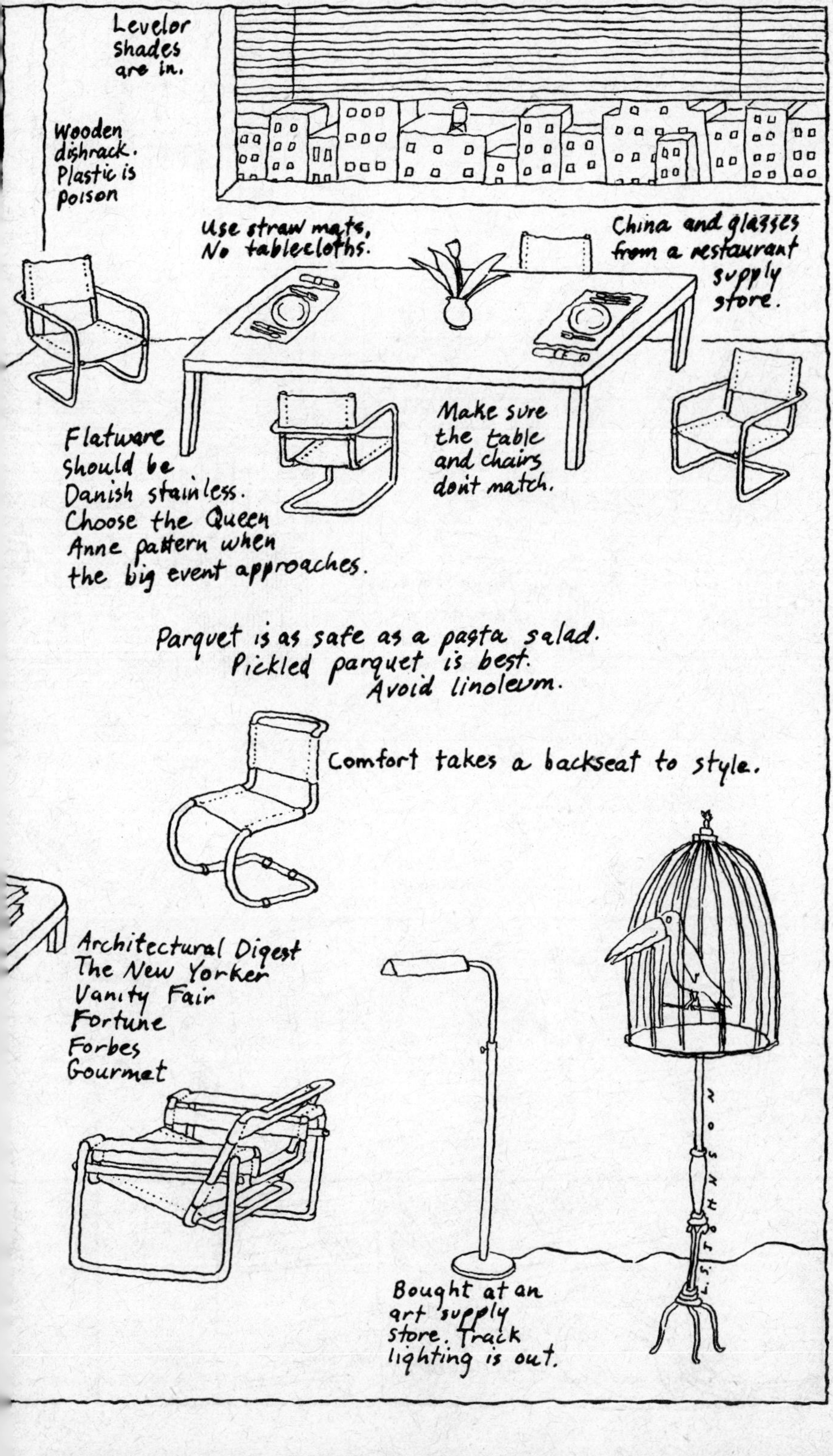
Levelor shades are in.
Wooden dishrack. Plastic is poison
Use straw mats, No tablecloths.
China and glasses from a restaurant supply store.
Flatware should be Danish stainless. Choose the Queen Anne pattern when the big event approaches.
Make sure the table and chairs don't match.
Parquet is as safe as a pasta salad. Pickled parquet is best. Avoid linoleum.
Comfort takes a backseat to style.
Architectural Digest
The New Yorker
Vanity Fair
Fortune
Forbes
Gourmet
Bought at an art supply store. Track lighting is out.

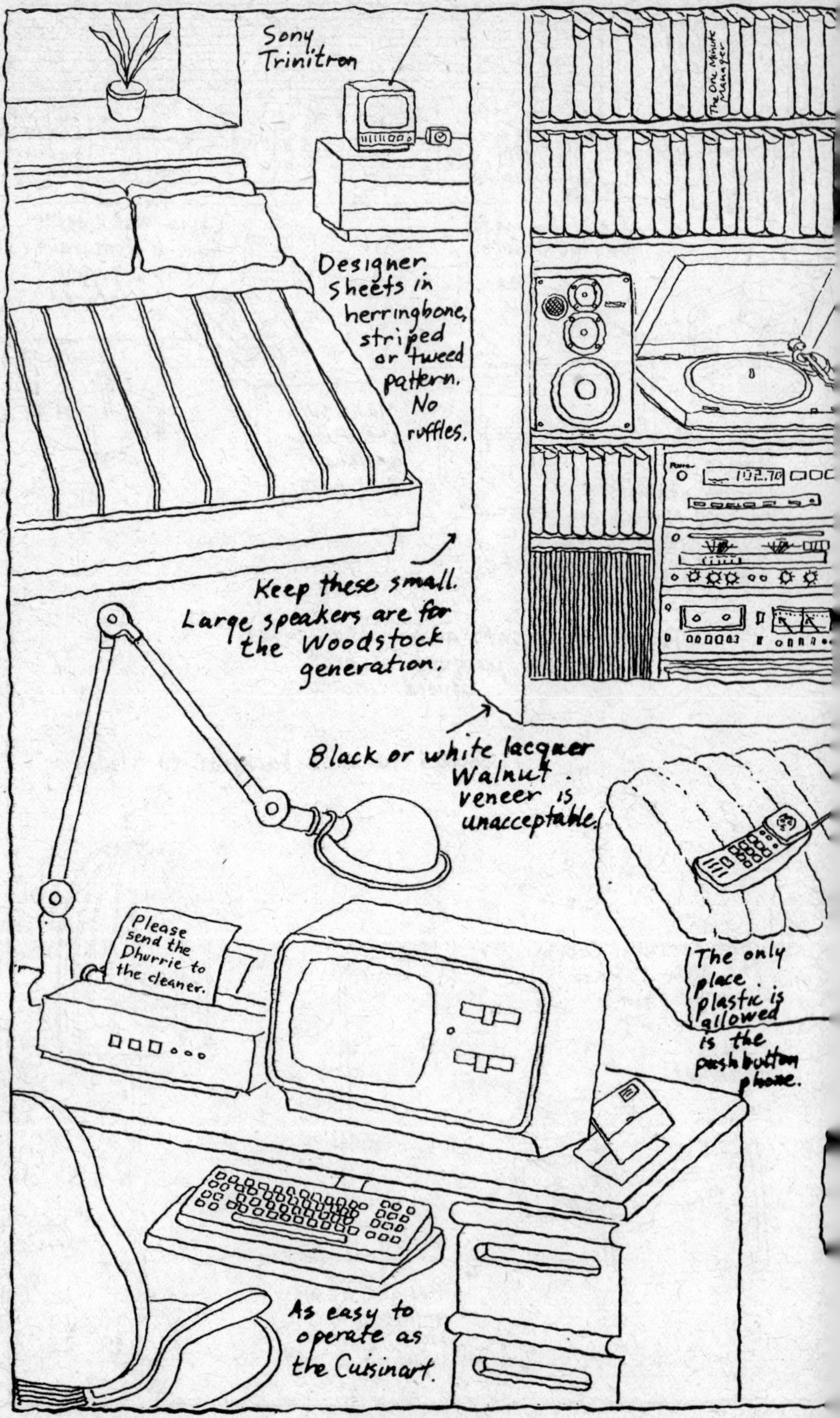
Sony Trinitron
The One Minute Manager
Designer Sheets in herringbone, striped or tweed pattern. No ruffles.
Keep these small. Large speakers are for the Woodstock generation.
Black or white lacquer. Walnut veneer is unacceptable.
Please send the Dhurrie to the cleaner.
The only place plastic is allowed is the push button phone.
As easy to operate as the Cuisinart.

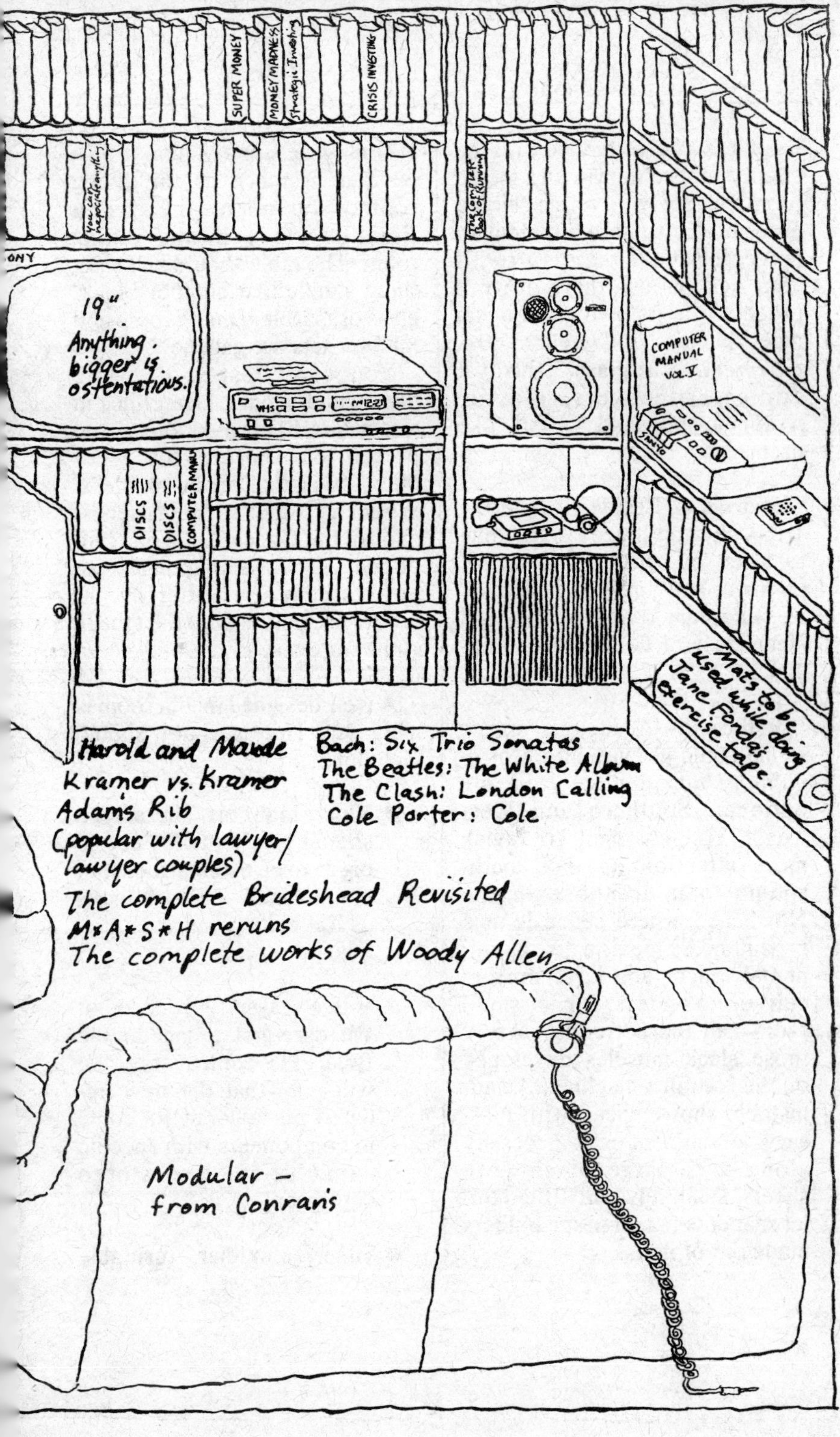

SUPER MONEY
MONEY MADNESS
Strategic Investing
CRISIS INVESTING
The Complete Book of Running
19"
Anything bigger is ostentatious.
VHS
COMPUTER MANUAL VOL. V
SANYO
DISCS
DISCS
COMPUTER MANU
Mats to be used while doing Jane Fonda's exercise tape.
Harold and Maude
Kramer vs. Kramer
Adams Rib
(popular with lawyer/lawyer couples)
The complete Brideshead Revisited
M*A*S*H reruns
The complete works of Woody Allen
Bach: Six Trio Sonatas
The Beatles: The White Album
The Clash: London Calling
Cole Porter: Cole
Modular – from Conran's

is, unless you've moved into the twenty-first century with a media room, where you've assembled enough electronic equipment to power the starship *Enterprise*. If your desk is also there, a word processor in its own gazebo is a nice touch. *No-Comment Department:* Cut-glass ashtrays, doilies, slipcovers, plastic-wrapped lampshades, and fake fireplaces.

Bedroom—Besides the Sony Trinitron, you'll need something to sleep on. Just get a simple platform bed and you're all set. By all means avoid ruffles, and steer clear of florals—too Preppie.

Bathroom—A Jacuzzi and/or sauna could get you into *Metropolitan Home,* but they're really optional. Southern and West Coast Yuppies tend to lavish more attention on their bathrooms than do those in the Northeast, where space is at a premium. A bidet is a nice Continental touch, and large mirrors can do wonders for a small room—all the better to gaze at those sleek muscles developed on the Nautilus machine. An adjustable shower head with massage attachment is a necessity along with large plush bath sheets. Definitely out: Tufted toilet seat covers and tissue holders made out of dolls.

Dining Room—If you don't have a fireplace in the living room, you might try a Ben Franklin stove in the dining room. The table should be something simple like butcher-block, glass or marble. Dining room and kitchen sets are gauche.

You can't lose with white dishes and simple, clean lines in glassware. Real silverware is too pretentious before the wedding—stick to Danish stainless. When the Big Event approaches, choose the Queen Anne pattern, of course, but keep your Danish for everyday use. After the divorce, use your half of the Queen Anne for everyday. You deserve it.

A well-designed media room is a big plus. Here's what it should include:

- Video monitor: The screen should be about 19″, not so big as to be ostentatious, but not so small so that it looks as if it belongs on your sailboat.

- Video cassette recorders: We dare not opine on the Beta/VHS controversy. We will note that the new updated portable VCRs come in components with specific capabilities, like stereo equipment.

- Tuner, amplifier, turntable

and tape deck: All should be neatly stacked. Of course, if you bought a digital disc player you could eliminate the turntable. (Before indulging, remember that the discs are so prohibitively priced, you'd think they were made of gold instead of copper.)

- Speakers: Keep them small; giant speakers are for the Woodstock generation.

- Personal computer terminal: The more sophisticated the model, the more impressive you will look while playing Cosmic Cruncher. If there's any possible chance you'll have some use for a word processor in the next ten years, buy one immediately. Make sure the printer is IBM Selectric quality so notes to your cleaning person will look like high-powered résumés.

- Solid-oak storage cabinets: Black or white lacquer is also fine, but stay away from walnut veneer.

- Storage racks: Should be of varying depths to accommodate your video cassettes, stereo cassettes, digital discs, computer programs and any record albums you may be keeping for nostalgia (early Dylans may never be available on digital discs).

- Shelves for your Walkman, Watchman, cordless phone, telephone answering machine with beeper, headphone, calculator and electronic toy collection.

- Stack of exercise mats to be used while doing Jane Fonda's Workout tape. ■

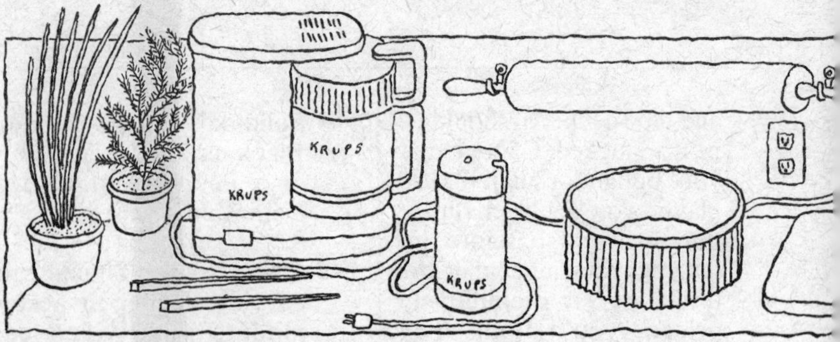

11. A Kitchen Quiz

THE KITCHEN is probably the most accurate reflection of one's Yuppie quotient. The following quiz should give you an idea of how secure your status is.

- Do you have a double sink? Add 3 points. After all, you need one side just to drain the pasta.
- Are all your kitchen appliances white or stainless steel? Add 5 points. Are they all almond? Add 3 points. Deduct 1 point for any appliance that's avocado or harvest gold. (Only deduct ½ point if the appliance is small enough to fit in a drawer.)
- Do you have a food processor? Add 0 points. Everybody has a food processor these days. Is the make a Robot Coupe? Add 2 points. A Cuisinart? Add 3 points. Do you have a large feed tube? Add 1 point. Do you have a julienne disk? Add ½ point.
- Add 1 point for anything that requires copper cleaner.
- Deduct 1 point for Teflon or non-stick pans.
- Add 2 points for all pans that cannot be washed in the dishwasher.

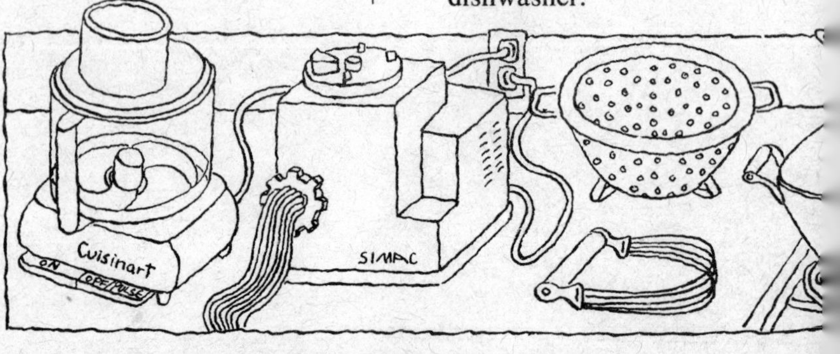

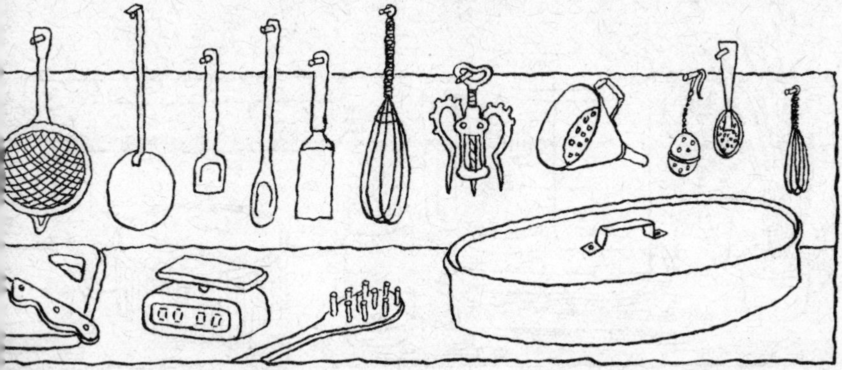

- Is there lighting underneath the cabinets so that no workspaces remain in the shadows? Add 2 points.
- Do you have a wok? Add 0 points. Do you have a couscousier? Add 2 points. Do you still have a fondue set? Deduct 1 point. It's taking up valuable storage space.
- Are the countertops butcher-block? Add 1 point. Do you have at least 2 square feet of countertop covered with marble for pastry and breadmaking? Add 3 points.
- Uninterrupted counter space counts for a lot. Are the stove, dishwasher, refrigerator and freezer all built into and under the counterspace? Add 3 points.
- Add ½ point for every piece of equipment hung on the wall or from an overhead rack. Functional decoration is very desirable.
- A stovetop griddle can be fabulous in a country kitchen, but seems contrived in town. Bacon, eggs and pancakes should be reserved for Sunday mornings in the woods. Add 1 point for the country house; deduct 1 point for the city.
- Industrial stoves are worth 2 points if they have stainless-steel range tops. Also add 1 point for every burner you have over 4 and every oven you have over 1.

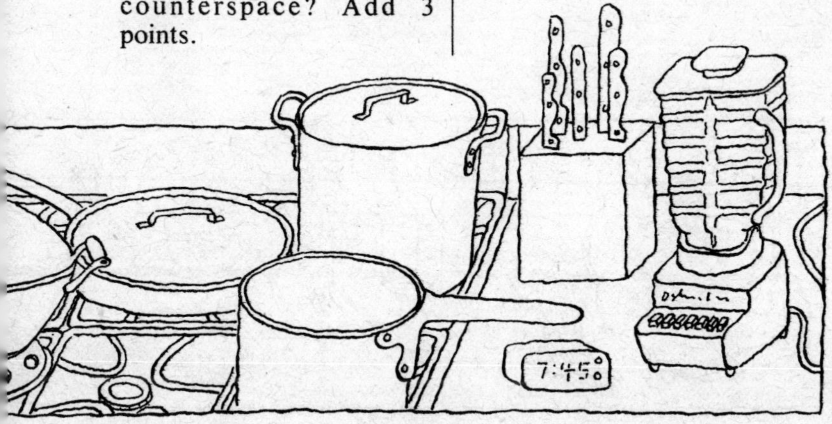

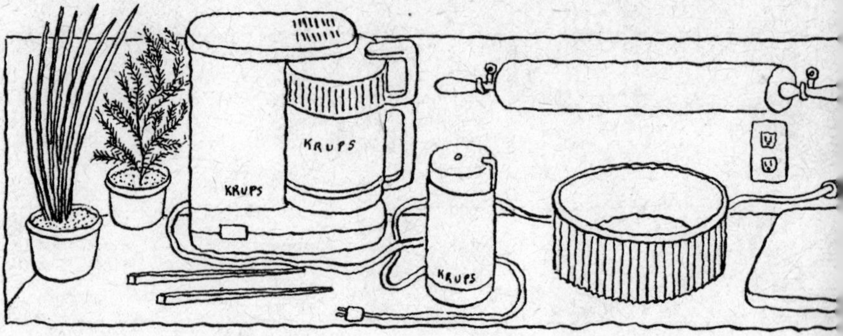

- Give yourself 1 point for every herb and spice visibly displayed, but deduct 1 for any of the following: garlic powder, onion powder, dehydrated onion flakes, MSG. Potted herbs are worth double.
- You get 1 point for any of the following: marble rolling pin, salmon poacher, bottle of vinegar containing actual vegetation.
- 1 point for every cutting knife, double if it was manufactured in Germany.
- Each cookbook is worth 1, double if it contains color photographic plates.
- Digital kitchen timer? One point.
- Subtract 4 points if your wine rack is in the kitchen. However, you can give yourself 2 points if you have one that can hold at least 48 bottles.
- Do you have a convection oven? Add 3 points. Does it have a grill? Add 1 point. A rotisserie? Add 1 point. A shish-kebab attachment? Add ½ point. A french fryer? Subtract 1 point. If you have a microwave oven, deduct 3 points. However, you need deduct only 2 if it has a browning element. At least the food looks decent, even if you do end up with cancer.

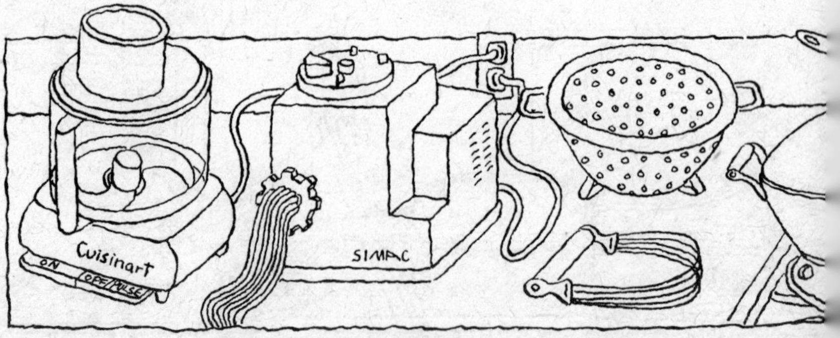

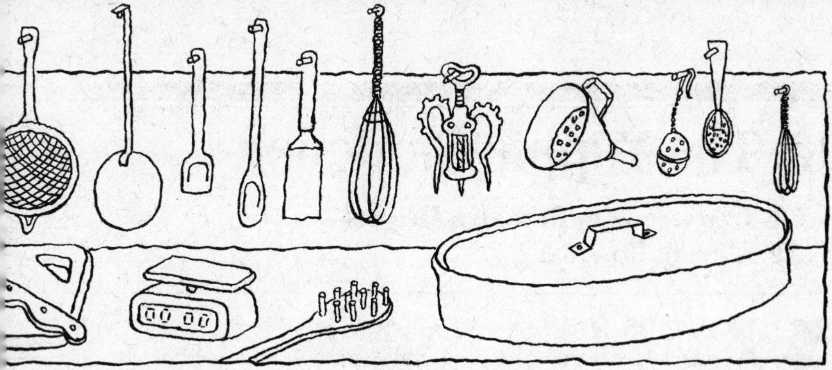

SCORING: If you have managed to score 50 points, you're a Super-Yuppie. By the way, a minimal amount of cheating is very Yuppie. Give yourself $1/4$ point extra for each bit of cheating you did. If it adds up to more than 2 points, though, subtract 3 and try to set yourself some limits in the future. ■

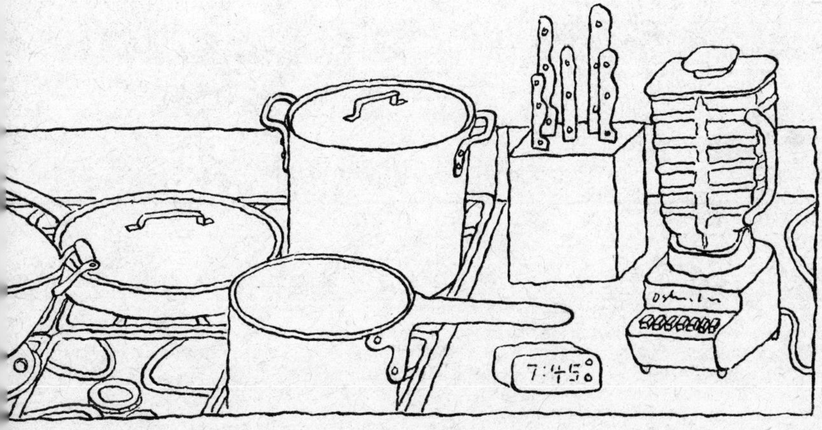

12. The Yuppie Gardener

A Fig Tree Grows in Brooklyn Heights—So Does Fresh Rosemary

YUPPIES HAVE herb gardens in their kitchen windows, fig trees in their living rooms and raise orchids as a hobby. A scented geranium or tasteful bromeliad (in bloom, of course) may grace a south window. Should you find yourself in a living room with snake plants and rubber trees, don't let the parquet floors fool you. It's definitely not a true Yuppie domicile.

Herewith, the very best—and worst—in the Yuppie botanical garden:

Genuine Yuppie	*Ersatz Yuppie*
bromeliads	snake plants
orchids	rubber trees
scented geraniums	philodendrons
herb gardens	avocado trees
Ficus benjaminas	marijuana

Other important points to remember when you are green-thumbing it:

1. Use as many ceramic glazed pots and antique brass planters as possible. If necessary, you may resort to an occasional unglazed clay pot. But stay away from plastic pots—they're as bad as plastic flowers. And whatever you do, don't ever plant anything in a coffee can. (Not only is it unattractive, but it's an announcement to the world that you're using canned coffee.)

2. An herb garden in the kitchen is an opportunity to show off your culinary sophistication as well as your gardening savvy. Stick to herbs that are used in Yuppie cuisine, the more esoteric the better. There's nothing more impressive than snipping fresh coriander leaves for a complicated Indian recipe, basil for your pesto, fresh tarragon to include in your vinaigrette or crushing your own anise seeds.

3. It's generally a good idea to stay away from any plant grown in your grandmother's apartment.* Snake plants in ceramic frogs won't do. If you must have a begonia, make sure it's a rex. Geraniums should be of the scented leaf variety.

4. Avocado pits are fun to sprout, but too unchallenging for today's urban gardener. Keep them in the kid's room.

5. Marijuana was fine to cultivate in your college dorm, but has no place in your condominium. Grow up.

6. Orchids are difficult to grow and therefore acceptable. If you're going to all the trouble of growing orchids, play it for all it's worth. Join your local orchid society and place their publication on your coffee table, beside several expensive photography books on the subject. Take color portraits of your blooms and frame them. If orchids seem to be too much of a production, try flowering bromeliads. Forcing bulbs is another alternative. ■

*Boston ferns are too corny for the true Yuppie windowsill, but maidenhair, bird's-nest, rabbit's-foot and staghorn varieties are temperamental enough to impress. Asparagus ferns should be confined to offices and restaurants.

13. State of the Arf

FOR THE YUPPIE who has never produced offspring, a pet makes the ideal child substitute. Even Yuppies who have children tend to treat their pet like a member of the family and another extension of the Yuppie ego.

Yuppies take their pets everywhere, from friends' apartments to the South of France by jet. A condo or summer home may be chosen for the facilities it offers the family cat or dog, and the animal's diet is as nutritionally sound and as aesthetically pleasing as any Yuppie youngster's. Pet owners interview for doggie obedience schools the way they would for their child's nursery school. The animal whose public behavior becomes unacceptably antisocial (e.g., chewing up the stereo headphones) will be sent to a pet therapist. And if a beloved pet should kick the bucket, the grieving Yuppie might seek out a practitioner of one of the newest Yuppie occupations—the social worker who specializes in pet-loss counseling.

The ultimate Yuppie puppy is the Akita, an overgrown chowlike beast that can cost more than $1,000. Its weekly food budget runs into double digits, but it serves as the perfect jogging companion and conversation piece. (Yuppies don't get out to bars as much as they used to, so conquests made while dog-walking often determine whether or not they have a date on Saturday night.)

Akitas are very big with Guppies, as are Dobermans in collars that match their owners'.

Yuppies with small living spaces or little time to walk the dog find cats are more convenient pets. Cats look equally ornate in brownstones and lofts, and are less likely than dogs to have an accident on the Oriental rug. One aspect of cat ownership that might have been a problem for Yuppies in the past—kitty litter smells—has been solved by the invention of the Yuppie cat box. It is covered with a hood, and filled with permanent litter made from charcoal pellets. The hottest Yuppie kitty is the Himalayan, which is furrier than a Siamese and more esoteric.

Those with serious allergies or painful memories of the destruction of a favorite piece of furniture by a former pet may find a fish tank appropriate. Of course, it must be a saltwater tank, and it must contain obscure and expensive varieties of tropical fish plus several specimens of sea anemones and live coral. In fact, if you want to do it right, you'll call in a gravel and coral consultant to make sure your tank is a showpiece worthy of standing next to your Brancusi reproduction. Or you may want to try an exotic bird. Macaws, toucans, cockatoos, mynas, parrots and finches should be chosen to complement your color scheme. And a brass antique bird cage can be as important a piece as a Le Corbusier chaise longue.

Stay away from turtles, salamanders, gerbils or parakeets, unless you have kids. ■

Naming the Beast

A pet's name must show imagination and knowledge. Since a Yuppie's career is so important, it's often the inspiration for a pet name. Here are some examples:

Psychiatry: Transference, Compulsion
Banking: Mortgage, Interest, Cee Dee
Business: Merger, Monopoly, Perks
Law: Arguendo, Habeas

To avoid arguments in two-career families with only one pet, it's best to use other aspects of Yuppie life as pet name material. For instance:

Favorite vacation spots: Aruba, Fiji and Galapagos (good for your kid's turtle)
Culinary terms: Kiwi, Chèvre, Julienne, Chanterelle
Yuppie heroes and heroines: Colette (for cats), Fonda, Bogie or Wolfgang (Mozart or Puck)

14. Yuppies on Wheels

THE TRUE YUPPIE, of course, rents garage space or hires someone else to park his car. The possible exception: the consultant or freelance who enjoys the challenge of parking on the street. These hardy souls must deal with street theft, of course. They do so by installing removable tape decks, intricate car alarms or a large sign in the back window proclaiming, "NO RADIO." Summer weekend car rentals are big in New York, where Yuppies who earn six-figures won't buy a car because of the hassles involved.

Whether buying, renting or leasing (popular on the West Coast), it's important to have a car that fits your self-image. The Yuppie image always combines good taste and good sense. ■

Yuppie auto choices are:

VW Rabbit (especially the convertible)
BMW
Volvo
Mercedes (small model only)
Pickup or Jeep (only if you have no use for one)
Saab

NOTE: If you live on the West Coast, buy something you can refer to as your "vehicle." ■

Do equip your car with:

Tape deck
Ski rack (even if you don't ski)
Radar detector
Eddie Bauer sheepskin seat covers

Stay away from:

Sponge dice hanging from the rear-view mirror
Raised rear ends
Fur-covered steering wheels

DIVERSIONARY PURSUITS

15. Out to Lunch

YUPPIES HAVE two week-day lunch options:

Option 1: Go to the gym and work out Pick up a plain yogurt (100 calories less than strawberry) on your way back to the office.

Option 2: Since you're going to the gym after work and will probably only have a yogurt for dinner, you can go to a Yuppie restaurant for a serious lunch. Yuppies with expense accounts always choose option 2. Lunch hours vary from industry to industry. Bankers and stockbrokers eat at noon. Lawyers eat at one or two (the probate department eats at one, litigators eat at two). Yuppies in the film industry eat at 3:30, no matter how early they came in. ■

Things Yuppies Eat for Lunch

Tuna Sashimi	Empanadas
Hunan Chicken	Pâté
Tortellini salad	Chef's Salad

Things Yuppies Don't Eat for Lunch

Tuna on White	Chicken Pot Pie
Chicken Chow Mein	Bologna
Macaroni and Cheese	Chef Boy-ar-dee Ravioli

16. Eating Out

Things you *will* find in a Yuppie restaurant:

Ceiling fans
Dark green walls with white tin ceilings
Dishes that require the use of unusual mushrooms
Exotic flowers, especially various types of lilies
Menus that describe desserts as being served with chantilly, instead of whipped cream
Amateur but friendly service by people with graduate degrees in everything but the culinary arts
Restrooms lined with mirrors
Black shiny surfaces
A piano player who specializes in "As Time Goes By"

Things you *won't* find in a Yuppie restaurant:

Restroom signs advising employees to wash their hands.
Placemats with crossword puzzles.
Friday night "All You Can Eat" fish fries.
Salad bars with macaroni salad and artificial bacon bits.
American cheese omelettes.
Waitresses named Millie, wearing short white dresses.
Menus that say the following:

Minimum at table—$2.50
Have A Nice Day!
Soup—Cup: 80¢/Bowl: $1.20
Please pay at register
No Substitutions
Column A and Column B
Visit our Passaic branch
All pies baked fresh today
Each additional topping: 25¢
Happy Hour: 5–7 P.M.
Thank you for your patronage ■

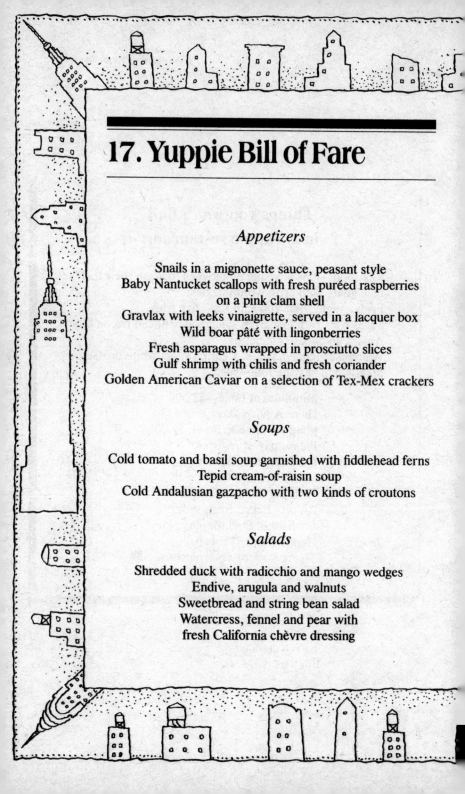

17. Yuppie Bill of Fare

Appetizers

Snails in a mignonette sauce, peasant style
Baby Nantucket scallops with fresh puréed raspberries on a pink clam shell
Gravlax with leeks vinaigrette, served in a lacquer box
Wild boar pâté with lingonberries
Fresh asparagus wrapped in prosciutto slices
Gulf shrimp with chilis and fresh coriander
Golden American Caviar on a selection of Tex-Mex crackers

Soups

Cold tomato and basil soup garnished with fiddlehead ferns
Tepid cream-of-raisin soup
Cold Andalusian gazpacho with two kinds of croutons

Salads

Shredded duck with radicchio and mango wedges
Endive, arugula and walnuts
Sweetbread and string bean salad
Watercress, fennel and pear with fresh California chèvre dressing

Pasta

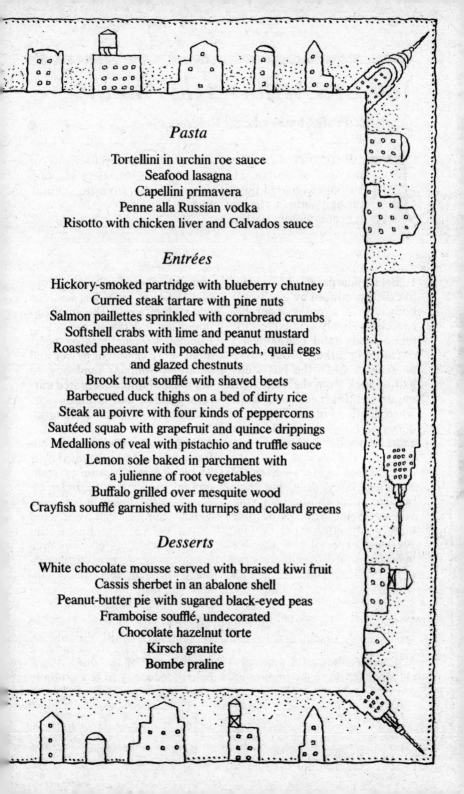

Tortellini in urchin roe sauce
Seafood lasagna
Capellini primavera
Penne alla Russian vodka
Risotto with chicken liver and Calvados sauce

Entrées

Hickory-smoked partridge with blueberry chutney
Curried steak tartare with pine nuts
Salmon paillettes sprinkled with cornbread crumbs
Softshell crabs with lime and peanut mustard
Roasted pheasant with poached peach, quail eggs
and glazed chestnuts
Brook trout soufflé with shaved beets
Barbecued duck thighs on a bed of dirty rice
Steak au poivre with four kinds of peppercorns
Sautéed squab with grapefruit and quince drippings
Medallions of veal with pistachio and truffle sauce
Lemon sole baked in parchment with
a julienne of root vegetables
Buffalo grilled over mesquite wood
Crayfish soufflé garnished with turnips and collard greens

Desserts

White chocolate mousse served with braised kiwi fruit
Cassis sherbet in an abalone shell
Peanut-butter pie with sugared black-eyed peas
Framboise soufflé, undecorated
Chocolate hazelnut torte
Kirsch granite
Bombe praline

18. *Les Artifices du Paradis*

(or PDR: Professional's Drug Reference)

FOR TODAY'S Yuppie, the use of intoxicants has taken on a purposeful and serious character completely unlike the hedonistic thrill-seeking of the 60s and 70s. Here's a rundown of the favorite Yuppie highs.

1. **Beta endorphine**—Morphine-like drug produced by one's own body after 20 minutes of aerobic exercise. Highly addictive. Effects: easily (and obnoxiously) outrunning other prospective passengers when the bus stops half a block from the stop sign; vague restlessness and guilt when deprived of the drug; tendency to buy multiple designer exercise outfits; euphoria.

2. **Designer waters**—Strictly speaking, not a drug, but their placebo effect can be very convincing. Some Yuppies become quite giddy after three or four Perriers, especially if they've been consumed over the course of a business lunch. As with wines, domestic varieties are growing in popularity, but steer clear of anything bottled in New Jersey.

3. **Cocaine**—Powerful aphrodisiac since its presence implies an atmosphere of easy money. Popular at discos, recording sessions and market week. The amphetamines are a déclassé substitute. Effects: a (sometimes exaggerated) sense of verbal power and acuity; insomnia; tendency to purchase multiple decorated mirrors, grinding and sifting devices and minuscule spoons; euphoria.

4. **Expensive caffeine**—Whether fresh-ground and consumed over *The Wall Street Journal* or fresh-ground and taken with lemon peel and the latest liqueur, the "high" here is that wide-eyed sense of having chosen the proper blend, and of being able to stay awake forever (there's so much to be done). Effects: Inability to fully open one's eyes in the morning without a dose of the drug, and an equally inappropriate inability to fully close one's eyes at night without a dose of one of the drugs listed below; tendency to buy multiple

expresso machines, etc.; euphoria. NOTE: Water-processed gourmet decaffeinated coffee, fresh-ground, has been used successfully in detox efforts.

5. **White wine**—Still big, but losing market share to red. Sparkling whites are bigger than ever.

6. **Red wine**—A new era is dawning. Now's the time to take that course in wine tasting. Expense can surpass even that of cocaine.

7. **Good dope**—Use limited to that segment of the Yuppie population which is unable to afford cocaine, too busy to jog or endowed with a certain sense of history—except for its mandatory enjoyment during hiking expeditions in the High Sierras.

8. **Valium**—True Yuppies always keep a supply on hand. Remember when Burt Reynolds asked for some in *Starting Over?* Besides, the famous muscle relaxant has so many respectable uses—menstrual cramps, the ever-present Yuppie back pain, even insomnia (after an especially late night at the office, of course). ■

19. Y.U.

WHEN THE self-improvement urge becomes overwhelming, to the point where the Yuppie is no longer content with increasing his muscle-to-fat ratio, he takes courses.

Although bread-and-butter classes in real estate taxes are universally *de rigueur,* Sausalito Yuppies tend to supplement them with more esoteric New Age subjects, like "Experiencing Your Plants on the Astral Plane." In New York, New School photography classes have given way to socially practical studies such as: "What to Do When Your Shrink Is On Vacation," "Avoiding Herpes," and "Chutzpah—How To Get Anything from Anyone, Anytime, Every Time."

Here's a brief rundown of other popular offerings embraced by Y.U. students.

The Cuisinart Seder

This one-session course, offered only in March, will teach you how to prepare a Passover feast like your grandmother used to make in a fraction of the time. Using a food processor, you will learn how to produce the lightest matzoh balls and the tastiest gefilte fish. You will also learn how to avoid common pitfalls, such as overly processed charroses and chopped liver, by developing the proper "pulse rate."

Ruth Goldschmidt and Myra Seidelberg are the authors of *Your Cuisinart Goes Kosher!* They are also well-known for their popular seminar, "Recognizing Pork Fat From a Distance," which enjoys a large following among female converts to Judaism.

How to Read an Ethiopian Menu

Most people can find their way around a French or Italian menu without any problem. Very few, however, can tell the waiter how much berberé to put in their dish or order another plate of injera with any degree of confidence. This course will not only equip you with a basic Ethiopian culinary vocabulary, but provides an answer to the question "What's wott?"

Massawa Menelik is the proprietor of the most popular Ethiopian restaurant in town, The Tigre. He was trained in the finest professional kitchens in Addis Ababa. He has also written the book *How Ethiopians Can Pick Up American Girls*.

How to Get Your Pet into Commercials

This seminar is for owners of everything from Abyssinians to zebras. Learn where to find an agent and how to prepare a pet résumé. Bring your pet with you and it will be videotaped. The tape will then be replayed to analyze your pet's strong and weak points. Lists of veterinarians who prescribe animal sedatives are distributed. Please bring no more than one pet with you.

Jim Swift has been an animal agent for upwards of thirty-five years. He has represented three Lassies and two Morrises.

Restoring Antique Toilets

Even the most conscientious brownstone renovator may overlook an inauthentic toilet fixture. It's not unusual to find a perfectly restored Victorian bathroom with a brass lamp, floral wallpaper, a four-legged bathtub, an antique sink and a glaringly modern porcelain toilet. This course teaches you how to avoid such gaucherie and provides you with a period-by-period historical overview of the indoor toilet, beginning with Thomas Crapper, its inventor. You will learn to appreciate the Old World charm of an overhead tank and where to find antique wooden toilet seats.

Instructor Luisa Calabrese grew up in a sixteenth-century Italian palazzo, with nineteenth-century plumbing.

Professional Journal Writing

Ever wonder if you could capitalize on your scratchpad or turn the diary you keep for your therapist into a best-selling novel? If you're already taping or writing a journal, this course could help make you an instant celebrity. If not, it may inspire you to start jotting down every detail of your potentially lucrative life story. You'll learn all you need to know about selling the film rights to your personal correspondence and copyrighting your thoughts. Tips on how to organize your material and how to check "writer's overflow" will also be included.

Anais Nijinski is a Russian émigrée and pioneer in the field of modern journal-writing methods. She recently received the Golden Memo award for a play based on her collected shopping lists. Her techniques are taught in courses throughout the U.S. and in Europe.

Earlobe Massage

Your earlobes are actually a map of your body. This little-known art of earlobe massage was developed by a Japanese zen master in the seventeenth century and has been practiced in northern Japan ever since. This course helps enable you to relieve all types of bodily discomfort through use of finger pressure on your earlobes and the upper part of your jawbone. You will unleash the free-flowing energy in your body by the use of massage, aura balancing and visualization.

Guido Ponzini has been a student of earlobe massage since 1976, when he spent a year in Japan studying micro-computers. Before that, Guido owned his own pizza parlor in New York's Little Italy, where he specialized in kneading dough.

Hypnosis Negotiation

Used for centuries in various kinds of mind control, hypnosis is still a newcomer at the conference table, but it can be a valuable tool in negotiating sessions. This course explores how to practice this ancient art without anyone present being aware of it. Used properly, hypnosis can give new meaning to the term: Getting to Yes.

Karl Krupp learned the art of hypnotism from his father at an early age. He applied it at the poker table and used his winnings to send himself to business school. ■

20. Getting Cultured

CULTURE TO A Yuppie, like everything else, means keeping up with the latest. It means knowing the important film of the week; being seen with the "right" book on the beach or by the pool; having subscriptions to the symphony, the ballet, the opera or a theater repertory company (preferably all four). But even if a Yuppie does not read *the* book, see *the* film, or attend *the* event, he can always carry on an intelligent conversation about the reviews.

Although going to the movies is number one on the Yuppie's entertainment list, they can appreciate other art forms, given the right conditions. Here's a quick run down of some of the ways Yuppies get cultured:

Visual Arts: Yuppies only go to museum exhibits if they require advance tickets. It started with King Tut, followed by Picasso. Pre-opening showings get high marks. Gallery hopping on rainy afternoons is still popular, but openings are really something to talk about.

Theater: Even Broadway musicals—once the domain of aging suburban matrons—have succumbed to the Yuppie onslaught. Yuppified favorites include *A Chorus Line, La Cage aux Folles* (très Gup), *Dreamgirls, Sophisticated Ladies,* and *Nine* (or anything else by Tommy Tune).

Opera: Pavarotti and public television brought Yuppies into opera houses, and now little blue-haired ladies must scrap with ruthless fast-trackers for season tickets. If you do get a subscription and decide you don't like it, unused tickets make great birthday presents or trading cards for other cultural events. There's no point in going if you haven't read the libretto and listened to the record.

Dance: Regional dance companies and balletomanes are sprouting up as fast as renovated townhouses. All else being equal, at least a passing acquaintanceship with ballet—especially modern—can help distinguish the Yuppie from an imposter who thinks he can get by with perfect film attendance.

Music: Yuppies won't have anything to do with concerts unless they take place in the proper setting. The 1812 Overture must be heard out of doors while lying on a blanket, drinking white wine and eating brie. Jazz requires an intimate club with a cover charge and a two-drink minimum. Ribs and Lone Star beer have to be on the menu if a Yuppie is going to sit through a set of Country and Western, and Punk Rock palaces are only appropriate for slumming. ■

21. Yup and Away: A Yuppie Vacation Guide

YUPPIES ADORE the exotic and undiscovered. (What's the point of going somewhere if your mother has already been there?) The problem is that Yuppies tend to discover places at the same time other Yuppies are discovering them. It's not unusual for a Yuppie to drive through the night to some "undiscovered" inn only to find the dining room packed with MBAs ordering cassis sherbet for dessert. Or to charter a sailboat in the Caribbean and head for a deserted island, only to meet a member of the co-op board at the snorkel equipment rental office once they get there. Or to spend the afternoon smugly negotiating what they thought was a virgin ski slope in the Alps, only to find their squash partner already in the chalet, sipping coffee (with liqueur, of course). Or to find a member of their law school class on top of the Great Pyramid.

All this can be quite disillusioning and may force some Yuppies back to the conventional. For the Yuppie who has stopped trying, a place like the Hamptons can be very comforting. The Yuppie in defeat buys or rents a house that looks very much like every other beach house. The beach, of course, looks the same no matter where you sun. Everyone plays tennis at the same club, and eats duck at one restaurant and fish at another. Every now and then a Yuppie in the midst of a summer novel may get a strange look in her eye and contemplate trekking in the Himalayas next summer. The urge will pass, however, and the Yuppie will then turn back to the important things in life—like reserving court time.

No matter how many times you've run across your squash partner in some rarefied atmosphere miles from the court, at least one of the following seasonal trips is required. ■

Summer

Four-week vacation to one of the seven wonders of the ancient world (e.g., the Great Pyramid), an exotic island where neolithic culture is still practiced (Easter Island) or a continent with strange wildlife and raging waters (Australia)

Backpacking in the High Sierras

Rafting in the High Rockies

Two weeks at a classy beach (Fire Island, Big Sur, Nantucket)

Winter

One week at a ski resort in the Alps or Vail, Colorado

A weekend of cross-country skiing

One week at a Mexican or Caribbean beach resort (cruises are for retired people—Yuppies always fly)

One week sailing a chartered boat in tropical waters

Christmas in rural England (rural New England will do)

Carnival in Rio

Fall

Foliage tour of New England, with bed and breakfast at a "charming country inn"

Fishing trip to Montana, staying at a quaint hunting lodge (no hunting)

Grape harvest tour of Northern California

Spring

Cherry blossom time in Tokyo

Riverboat trip up the Mississippi

Fishing trip to the Smoky Mountains

Trip to the Cannes Film Festival ■

22. Yuppie Bestsellers: Books, Movies, Records

BOOKS

NON-FICTION:

1. **Getting by on $100,000 a Year,** by Andrew Tobias (most Yuppies can't)
2. **In Search of Excellence: Lessons from America's Best-Run Companies,** by Thomas J. Peters and Robert H. Waterman, Jr.
3. **Getting to Yes: Negotiating Agreement Without Giving In,** by Roger Fisher and William Ury (and anything else with two male authors and at least a sevenword title)
4. **Chez Panisse Menu Cookbook,** by Alice L. Waters
5. **The Silver Palate Cookbook,** by Julee Rosso et al.

FICTION:

1. **The White Hotel,** by D. M. Thomas (read by all Yuppies who have ever been in analysis)
2. **The Group,** by Mary McCarthy (read by Yuppettes during the college admission process)
3. **The World According to Garp,** by John Irving
4. **One Hundred Years of Solitude,** by Gabriel Garcia Marquez (just say it's your favorite book)
5. **Pride and Prejudice,** by Jane Austen (every Yuppie knows that Elizabeth Bennett would have gone to law school had she lived today)

MOVIES

1. **Annie Hall** (and anything else by Woody Allen)
2. **Breakfast at Tiffany's:** Audrey Hepburn lives beyond her means and George Peppard wears a Burberry trenchcoat in the final scene
3. **Casablanca:** Responsible for the proliferation of ceiling fans in Yuppie restaurants
4. **Chariots of Fire:** Focused on athletics, competitiveness and expensive clothing—three important Yuppie values
5. **Citizen Kane:** Based on the life of William Randolph Hearst, an early Yuppie role model who had the foresight to buy land in California
6. **The Graduate:** Yuppies still smile with recognition at the word "plastics"
7. **Jules and Jim:** Good assertiveness training for Yuppie women; also showed that the condo could be cheaper split three ways
8. **King of Hearts:** Demonstrates the possible dangers of missing too many therapy sessions
9. **Scenes from a Marriage:** Glimpse into the life of a two-career Swedish family
10. **Sophie's Choice:** Interesting look at a Victorian mansion before renovation
11. **An Unmarried Woman:** Excellent footage of Soho lofts

RECORDS

1. **Vivaldi: The Four Seasons,** transcribed for flute by James Galway
2. **"Empty Bed Blues,"** by Bessie Smith—Yuppies are fascinated by musical geniuses who died in miserable circumstances
3. **"Jalousie,"** by Yehudi Menuhin and Stephane Grappelli
4. Anything by **Peter Allen** of recent vintage (a Guppie discovery)
5. Soundtrack from any failed **Stephen Sondheim** musical
6. **Synchronicity,** by The Police (just to show you're still on the fast track)

SPECIAL INTEREST

For Buppies or Yuppies who are addicted to the Caribbean: anything by Jimmy Cliff or Bob Marley

For avant-garde Yuppies: any artist who uses as many media as possible (e.g., Philip Glass, Laurie Anderson, the Paul Winter Consort) ■

23. Organized Religion

YUPPIES HAVE their own form of organized religion. They invariably worship at the altar of self-improvement. And they're *very* organized about it.

Rituals include:

- Weekly confessionals at the psychotherapist
- Religious education classes at a Yuppie adult education center
- Daily sunrise devotionals in the running track
- Adherence to a strict dietary code: No processed foods; no dessert before aerobics, etc.

Sabbath

Regardless of upbringing, many Yuppies find themselves working a half day on Saturday. This leaves Sunday as the only option for the Yuppie Sabbath, a day devoted entirely to self-worship.

Orthodox Yuppies usually begin Sabbath observances at sundown on Saturday with a ritual dinner party during which the hosts lead the guests in paying homage to the gods and goddesses of New American cooking, estate-bottled wines and designer evening wear. Reform Yuppies may simply join friends at a Yuppie restaurant, before or after a Yuppie cultural event.

Orthodox Yuppies are up bright and early Sunday morning for even more intense than usual exercise. "The extra mile" to a Yuppie means at least five more than weekdays. Sailing, tennis, cross-country skiing, hiking and ice skating may be substituted for jogging. The more casual reform Yuppie will sleep late on Sundays based on the doctrine that one's beautiful Yuppie body—having exercised all week—needs extra rest, not extra jogging.

All branches of the faith reserve late Sunday morning for the reading of religious texts: real estate and business sections of the Sunday newspaper and articles on the three F's (food, fashion, furnishings) from the Sunday magazine section.

At noon Yuppies don their most casual and most flamboyant designer clothes (jogging suits, jeans, caftans, etc.) in preparation for Holy Communion. This involves partaking of the holy sacraments—champagne and brioche—during a ceremony called brunch. Brunch may be observed at home with several guests or in an appropriate Yuppie restaurant. Musical accompaniment is important. This can be a classical guitar, but high mass requires a string quartet. Reform services favor jazz combos. In good weather, brunch is often held out-of-doors—in a sidewalk cafe or private yard. In winter, a roaring fire is *de rigueur*.

A Yuppie most nearly approaches sainthood when he or she is able to accomplish more things in a single day than is humanly possible. On the Sabbath, the devout Yuppie makes an extra effort in this direction. Brunch, for example, may be observed two, three, even four times, since its appointed hours stretch from before noon to after four. The multiple brunch is often combined with pilgrimages to the ski lodge or country house, especially on High Holy Days—three-day weekends occasioned by federal holidays. Between brunches, good Yuppies try to schedule some shopping, perhaps a movie, a little self-improvement reading or anything else that will keep them on the fast track that leads to the wrought iron gates of Yuppie heaven.

The only thing lacking in Yuppie religion is a full-fledged Yuppie Bible—so we wrote this book. ■

The Yuppie ten commandments are:

I

Thou shalt have no other gods before thyself.

II

Thou shalt take unto thee only designer labels.

III

Thou shalt always speak the name of thy wine merchant and the name of thy cleaning person with reverence.

IV

Thou shalt remember to have brunch on Sunday.

V

Honor thy investment banker and thy real estate agent.

VI

Thou shalt not kill whales or baby seals (save murder for the stock market).

VII

Thou shalt not commit adultery with thy boss.

VIII

Thou shalt not steal. Your lawyer is a pro at it—that's why you have one.

IX

Thou shalt not wear false materials, neither polyester nor vinyl; nor serve false consumables, neither Cool Whip nor Tang.

X

Thou shalt not covet thy neighbor's southern exposure. (If you'd paid $10,000 extra for the co-op, you could have had one, too.)

24. Mail-Order Mania

WHAT'S THE PERfect insomnia cure for Yuppies when Sominex, red wine and Mary Tyler Moore reruns won't work? They whip out their charge cards and dial 1–800, because that stack of catalogs on the coffee table can do what sleeping pills can't. Once the urge to acquire strikes at 2:00 A.M., it will gnaw at the Yuppie soul until an order has been placed. The true Yuppie, always on the fast track to materialism, gleefully succumbs to mail-order mania.

It's the middle of the night and our Yuppie has the urge to buy. Like all authentic Yuppies, he demands instant gratification. What are his options? Forget Sears and Montgomery Ward. We're talking posh parcel post. Here are some possibilities:

Conran's: The best cure for Yuppie insomnia might be a new bed.

L. L. Bean: Bean's clientele was originally confined to genuine Preppies with at least one uncle who actually hunted ducks. These days, even Yuppies whose uncles made it big in the seltzer or mozzarella business order the Maine hunting shoe and wear it with pride.

Eddie Bauer: For those who consider Bean's to be for city slickers with rustic pretensions; try Bauer's Superior Polar Parka, guaranteed to keep you warm even above tree line.

Williams Sonoma: Kitchenware for the terminally esoteric; features croissant cutters, crustacean crushers and quail cutlery.

The Sharper Image: Gadgets for those who worship the digital; now you can take your temperature and get a reading to the third decimal place.

Hemmings Motor News: A listing of vintage cars; you can certainly order a Rolls-Royce Corniche, but the federal government will not permit them to ship the chauffeur by mail.

United Farm Agency: Tired of scouring the countryside for a charming weekend retreat? Select one from the pages of this catalog and you'll never have to house-hunt again.

Victoria's Secret: What *Playboy*

and *Penthouse* are to the beer and bowling set, this lingerie catalog is to the Yuppie set. Features wet lips, stray tendrils and lots of tastefully displayed cleavage.

The American Express Catalog: Sent to all cardholders. Keep it in full view since it gives the world a glimpse into your credit card case.

A warning to catalog voyeurs: Getting on the mailing list is simple; staying on is trickier. The computer will drop apostates, so try to order at least a trinket every now and then.

The Fashionable Yuppie

If they can find the time during waking hours, Yuppies love to spend money on clothes. However, Yuppie office wear does not lend itself to displaying impeccable taste or knowledge of current trends. The idea is to look as much like John Dean as possible, whether you're a man or a woman. Indeed, Yuppie women—through careful research and numerous lunch time seminars—have proven beyond any doubt that they can look just as boring as men.

But even the most conservative Yuppie eventually tires of sensible, natural fabrics from the fogged-in-at-Heathrow end of the color spectrum. When you get the urge to blow major money on clothes, remember that the health club is one of the best places to display your plumage. Exercise outfits come in a dazzling array of vivid colors and in a range of styles from neo-punk to the lace-trimmed baby doll look. Striped leotards have become especially popular since Jane Fonda lifted her leg on the front of her workout book. Matching accessories are even more fun to buy. For each outfit you'll need socks, leg warmers, sweatbands, headbands, tote bags, even fingerless gloves to protect your hands while working out on the nautilus.

Outdoor sports such as skiing, tennis, backpacking, and windsurfing call for top-of-the-line clothing and equipment of the latest scientific design. The knowledgeable Yuppie can casually toss off words like gortex and thinsulate as effortlessly as he can discuss natural sources of Vitamin A. Be sure you purchase your equipment at a fine sporting goods store staffed by knowledgeable salespeople. In other words, never buy a backpack at K-Mart from a salesgirl wearing fingernail polish. ■

25. The Ultimate Crossword

Across

1. Use a Cross pen instead of this
2. Yuppie puppy
7. Degree received from 29 across
9. Yuppie direction
12. Body sculpture equipment
14. Only an Amex gold one will do
15. Chair for butcher-block table
16. Heartbreak of the Boston Marathon
18. Yuppie word for choose
20. Extra support for running shoes
25. Being a Yuppie means never having to say you're ______
26. Yuppie saving bank
27. ______ Hill, historic Yuppie neighborhood
29. Oxford of Yuppie education
31. Yuppie film classic
33. Advice for Yuppies with running injuries
37. Obligatory wristwear
38. Ingredient in 19 down
39. Disease contracted in a Japanese restaurant

Down

1. Verb meaning to eat on Sunday
3. Yuppiest of fruits
4. Yuppie winter vacation spot
5. Used in 21 down
6. Yuppie form of home ownership
8. Beyond peanut butter
10. Yuppie trenchcoat
11. ______ endorphine, Yuppie drug
13. Predecessor of plastic
17. Yuppie member of the onion family
19. Sauce made with 38 across
21. Yuppie summer vacation spot
22. Arugula on the Yuppie scale
23. What Yuppies don't do, except during 31 across
24. Favorite Yuppie sitcom
27. Tuna salad à la Yuppie
28. How Yuppies do everything
30. Use for 19 down
32. Granny Smith is a Yuppier version than delicious
34. Only on your legs, not on your cucumber
35. Eaten only in the form of barbecued ribs
36. Chèvre's mom

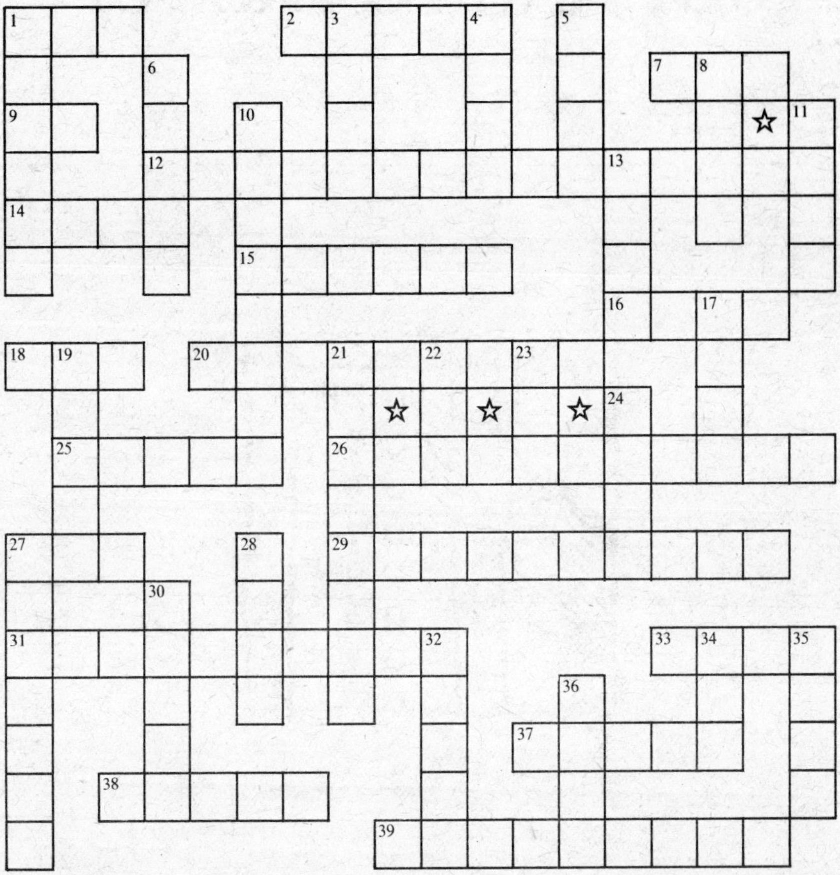

ANSWERS

Across: 1. Bic 2. Akita 7. MBA 9. Up 12. Nautilus machine 14. Card 15. Breuer 16. Hill 18. Opt 20. Orthotics 25. Sorry 26. Money Market 27. Nob 29. The B School 31. Casablanca 33. Swim 37. Rolex 38. Basil 39. Hepatitis

DOWN: 1. Brunch 3. Kiwi 4. Alps 5. Paba 6. Condo 8. Brie 10. Burberry 11. Beta 13. Cash 17. Leek 19. Pesto 21. Hamptons 22. Ten 23. Cry 24. Mash 27. Niçoise 28. Well 30. Pasta 32. Apple 34. Wax 35. Meat 36. Goat

GETTING TO THE TOP

26. A Day in the Life of a Yuppie

A.M. 7:00 Digital alarm clock goes off. It is programmed to play a cassette of Pachelbel's Canon in D Minor.

7:02 Krupps coffee machine turns on automatically, while Jennifer rewinds Jane Fonda Workout videotape.

7:03 Jennifer breezes through advanced segment while Michael lathers up with a natural boar bristle brush and Crabtree & Evelyn shaving soap in a wooden bowl.

7:30 They take turns showering. Both use the most powerful setting on the shower massage.

7:56 Michael and Jennifer drink their coffee while donning their respective single-vented navy blue suits. Jennifer puts on Adidas over her stockings and tucks her pumps into her briefcase. Michael wears his wingtips.

8:05 Jennifer picks up *The Wall Street Journal* and boards the subway. Michael buys the daily newspaper and walks to the office.

8:30 Arriving at their separate offices, they eat breakfast at their desks. Michael has a croissant with jam, no butter. Jennifer munches on a toasted bagel with butter, no jam.

9:10 Jennifer calls Michael to discuss the dinner party they're having that night for their Guppie friends, Bruce and Bob. He's away from his desk.

9:20 Michael returns Jennifer's call.

M: I know what we should serve Bob and Bruce for dinner tonight—mesquite-grilled eels. I just read a recipe in the *Lifestyle* section and it sounds wonderful.

J: Terrific. The B's love seafood. I'll decide on the wine. Talk to you later.

Michael and Jennifer spend the rest of the morning revising their respective memos. Michael is working on the third draft of his memo on utility mergers. Jennifer is on her fourth draft of a memo on utility divestitures.

P.M. 12:30 Jennifer ducks into a sidewalk health food bar for a quick bite, and spends her lunch hour at a seminar for executive women, which concerns the lack of advancement opportunities for male secretaries.

1:00 Michael grabs lunch at a sidewalk clam bar and spends the rest of the hour tracking down mesquite.

2:10 Michael calls Jennifer. She's in conference.

2:30 Jennifer returns his call.

J: Does Steven still have our tape of Sherpa music? We could show Bob and Bruce our slides from the Himalayas.

M: No, Steven hasn't sent back the tape yet, and you know the slides just wouldn't be the same without it. Why don't we show them our documentary on Sony at obedience school? You know their little Kenzo is interviewing now.

J: Fine. Meet you on the court at six.

Jennifer and Michael continue working on their memos for the rest of the afternoon.

3:37 Cleaning lady calls Michael to ask where she should send the Dhurrie rug to be cleaned. He tells her to wait until next week because of the party.

3:45 Stockbroker calls Jennifer to see if she's interested in hot new municipals.

5:30 Jennifer and Michael leave work and race to the racquet club.

7:03 Jennifer beats Michael by a narrow margin.

M: I guess I'll have to work on my strategy.

J: That's all right. I love to win. How about Napa Valley Chardonnay with the eels?

M: Sounds excellent. See you soon.

7:37 Jennifer leaves wine shop and heads for gourmet deli.

7:45 Michael finds fish store is out of eels and tries another one two blocks away.

7:58 Michael and Jennifer arrive at home in separate cabs, kiss and check their watches.

8:04 Jennifer and Michael finish emptying an array of appetizers from cartons onto Fiesta serving dishes.

8:14 Bob and Bruce arrive bearing a bouquet of day lilies, small orchids and a bird of paradise.

8:24 Bob helps Michael start the mesquite fire on the roof garden, while Bruce helps Jennifer with the Kir Royales.

8:35 The four of them munch gravlax, leeks vinaigrette and vegetable pâté as they watch the eels grill. A Scarlatti sonata accompanies their conversation from the outdoor speakers.

9:37 When dinner is over, the four of them play "The Cleaning Person Did It," a new murder mystery game, on the computer.

10:43 After a Courvoisier nightcap, Bob and Bruce head for the door. Everyone exchanges a kiss on the cheek. (Bruce works in the theater.)

10:52 Michael and Jennifer undress and prepare to retire.

J: (From the bathroom) "Do we have time for sex tonight, dear?"

M: "No, not tonight. It's late and we have to be at couples therapy by 7:30 tomorrow morning."

11:02 Michael sets the alarm for 6:30 A.M. "Night, darling." They kiss. (Fade out) ■

27. The Yupscale: How to Evaluate a Job

INTERESTING WORK and a solid five-figure salary are only two aspects of the right Yuppie job. It must also sound impressive at dinner parties and be open to exploitation in the media. If the job provides feature material for the six o'clock news or the style section of the newspaper, so much the better. Here then is the way various professions and career specialties stack up, on a scale of 1 to 10.

Lawyer	6
Corporate lawyer who specializes in takeovers	8
Divorce lawyer who rates an article in *People* magazine	10
Banker	5
Investment banker	6
Banker who handles Steven Spielberg's investments	9
Therapist	4
Therapist with a group	6
Therapist with two celebrity clients	8
Therapist with a syndicated column or book	9
Chef	3
Pastry chef	6
Frostier	7

MBA at a Fortune 500 company	5
MBA who could be quoted in *Forbes* Magazine	7
MBA who's an executive at a movie or record company	8
Nurse	2
Psychiatric nurse	4
Nurse who writes medical thrillers	7
Doctor	6
Sports medicine doctor	7
Doctor who has switched to commodity trading	9
Restaurateur	4
Restaurateur with a *nouvelle cuisine* restaurant	6
Elaine	10
Hairdresser	1
Hairdresser who cuts Jill Clayburgh's hair	3
Hairdresser who's now a movie producer	8
Newspaper reporter	5
Investigative journalist	7
Gossip columnist	8
Computer programmer	5
Systems analyst	7
Programmer who's invented a new computer	9
Graphic artist	4
Interior decorator	6
Interior decorator who guarantees a feature in *Architectural Digest*	9

28. The Workspace

ONCE UPON a time, not too long ago, Yuppies still had offices, and a title on the door rated an Oriental on the floor. The modern Yuppie now has a "workspace" instead, which consists of wall-to-wall industrial carpeting, upon which rest a few, modular chairlike forms covered in grey flannel, and an open work station *sans* door. The old rules obviously no longer apply. Forget about diplomas and bulletin boards on the wall. For the up-and-coming Yup faced with designing his own workspace, it helps to know the jargon ("workspace" instead of office is only the beginning). Herewith, a glossary of terms:

Task lighting: Variable intensity provides just the right light for any job. Also known as fast track lighting.

Modular furniture systems: Designed to be disassembled and moved for specific projects, they're also handy for corporate mergers and quick reorganizing under Chapter 11 bankruptcy proceedings.

Computer support furniture: Don't think about bookcases, desks and chairs. Your computer needs more support than your back. Furniture for use with computers must achieve "maximum effective machine integration." In other words, your furniture and your Apple II are almost indistinguishable.

Ergonomic seating: Ergonomics is the study of the human body in relation to the physical environment, especially in the workplace. Ergonomic seating is simply jargon for a comfortable desk chair.

Open-plan work station: Partitions are the contemporary alternatives to walls. The higher the partition, the more important the employee being partitioned. If your partition panel measures 68″, you're okay, but a panel of under 48″ might be an indication of slow tracking. Open-plan work stations are becoming so prevalent that new terms had to be invented for the office as we used to know it. If you're high enough on the corporate ladder to have an office with walls, you must refer to it as an "enclosed office." Your walls are known as "ceiling height partitions" and should you be lucky enough to have a four-legged desk, you're writing on something known as "freestanding furniture."

Once you've got the terminology down, you're ready to hire a workspace designer (formerly known as an interior decorator). If you've got a big design budget, you should shop at Roche, Atelier International, Knoll or anywhere that you can't get into without a professional. Here's what surrounds the rich and powerful as they doodle on their desk blotters and stare out of the window:

- A pedestal desk with polished chrome base and a marble top containing a leather inset instead of a desk blotter.

- An executive desk chair upholstered in Hermes or Connelly leather. (That's the stuff they use for Rolls-Royces. The perfection of the leather is attributable to the fact that they don't fence their cows in with barbed wire.) Varieties include Ward Bennetts' Mobius chair, Knoll's classic Pollack chair and Herman Miller's Ergon chair. (Just make sure your chair has *someone's* name attached to it.)

- For visitors, Corbusier's La Grande Confort is nice when done in museum-grade leather. The same goes for Mies van der Rohe's Barcelona chair and Marcel Breuer's Cesca chair. Whichever you choose, an L-shaped sofa in matching leather with a glass and chrome coffee table is *de rigueur.*

- Walls made from glass block laid like masonry and shaped into curved planes look as good in offices as they did in 1950s motel bathrooms.

- Edward Fields, the ultimate in carpets for the workspace, makes what they call pure wool corporate fantasies. For a higher-tech look, ceramic tiles work well or—if the cleaning staff is truly outstanding—why not a genuine leather tile floor?

- Office plants in chrome planters are important design elements, but don't trust your workspace designer for this; hire an "office landscaper."

- Framed posters are only one step removed from unframed posters. Do you think Malcolm Forbes has *New Yorker* Magazine covers on his walls? Only limited edition lithographs will do. ■

29. Income Wheel

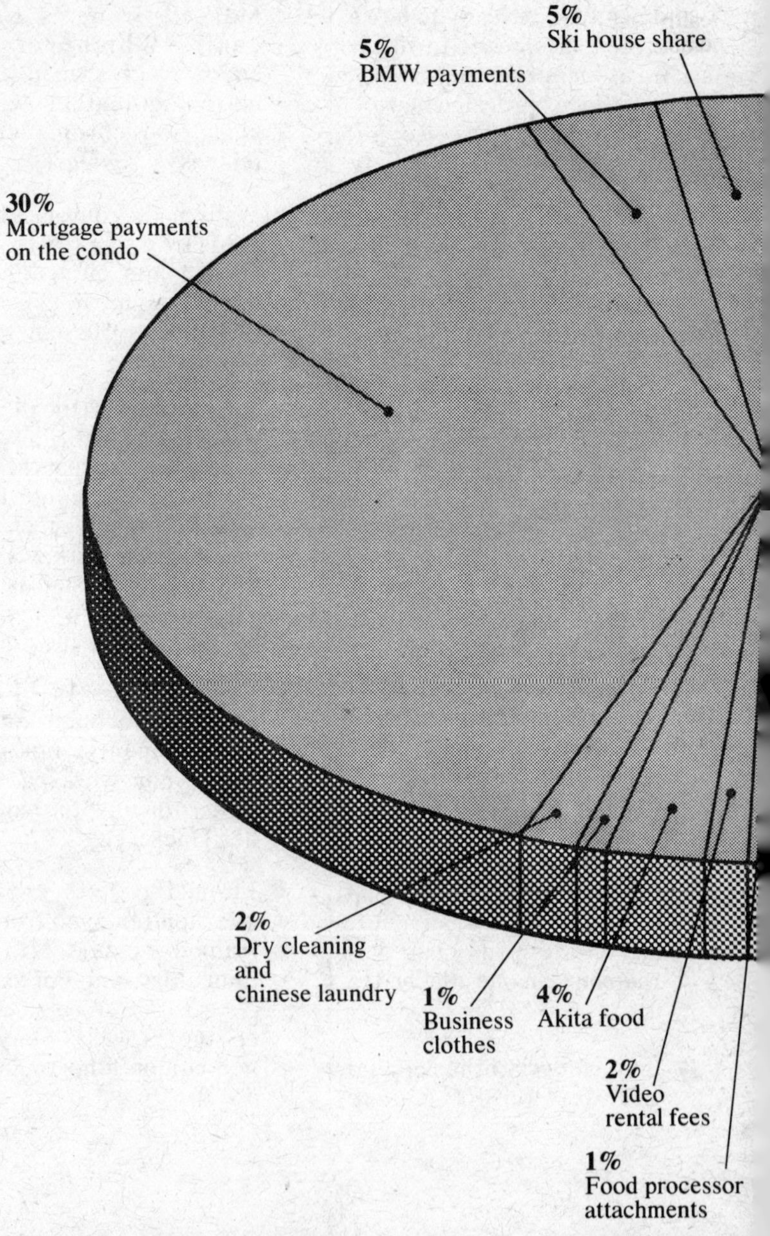
5%
Ski house share
5%
BMW payments
30%
Mortgage payments
on the condo
2%
Dry cleaning
and
chinese laundry
1%
Business
clothes
4%
Akita food
2%
Video
rental fees
1%
Food processor
attachments

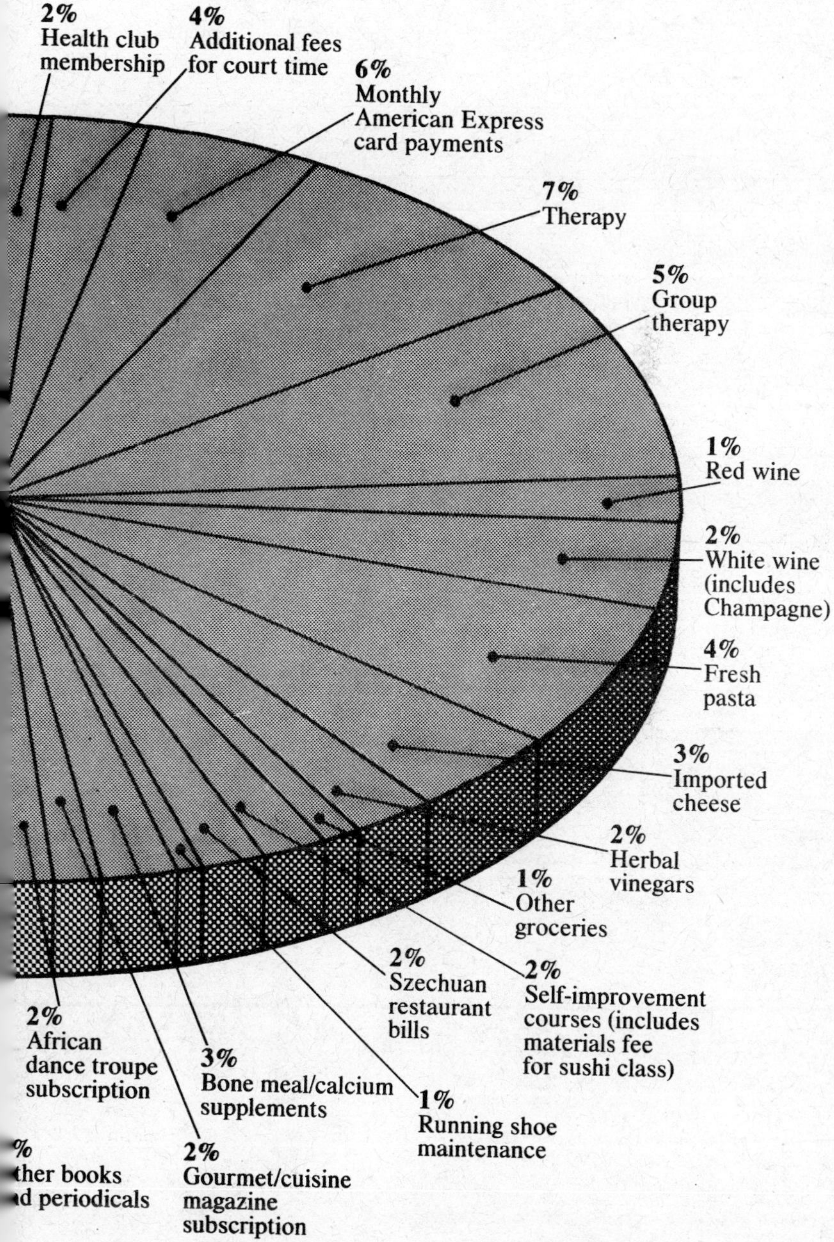
2% Health club membership
4% Additional fees for court time
6% Monthly American Express card payments
7% Therapy
5% Group therapy
1% Red wine
2% White wine (includes Champagne)
4% Fresh pasta
3% Imported cheese
2% Herbal vinegars
1% Other groceries
2% Self-improvement courses (includes materials fee for sushi class)
2% Szechuan restaurant bills
1% Running shoe maintenance
3% Bone meal/calcium supplements
2% Gourmet/cuisine magazine subscription
2% African dance troupe subscription
% ther books d periodicals

PERSONAL INTERFACING

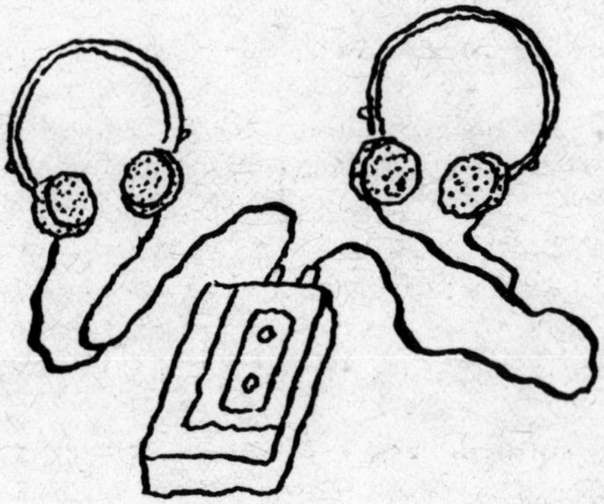

30. It's Only Yuppie Love

YUPPIES DON'T love their lovers. They love Vivaldi, their new apartments and the color of the ocean off St. Thomas in January. They have *relationships* with their lovers, which come in three stages:

1. Getting into the relationship—much like getting into a canoe.

2. Working on the relationship—much like working on your tax returns.

3. Ending the relationship—a simple matter since it's only Yuppie love.

Yuppies do marry (or buy a joint condo if gay) and tend to remain monogamous to avoid herpes. Although children are not in the forefront of Yuppie preoccupations, straight couples will consider a family if they have dovetailing schedules. The number of Yuppie children per family ranges from 0 to 1.

Notoriously short on time, Yuppies don't look for emotional riches in marriage. Instead, they view themselves as two well-educated, highly paid people coming together for the better life, lower housing costs and a combined annual income in the six figures. In fact, the marriage of two Yuppies is not unlike the merger of two corporations.

Even before the marriage takes place, Yuppies write their own corporate bylaws in the form of a prenuptial agreement. Thus, signing the marriage certificate is a mere formality, very much like signing a certificate of incorporation. The partners of the marriage have been known to pencil each other in for lunch, not unlike two corporate vice presidents. The joint tax return is so complicated, it's often thicker than an annual report. Since Yuppies train themselves to be competitive and "assertive," power struggles are inevitable. As anyone on Wall Street can tell you, there is only room for one at the corporate helm. If it's not true love, the unfortunate consequence is often a decree of dissolution.

Michael and Jennifer met at a gallery opening in Soho. It was a perfect evening—the moon was full and the mozzarella was smoked. Their initial conversation was promising. Of course, what they said bore little relationship to what they were actually thinking.

JENNIFER: The smoked mozzarella is excellent, don't you think? (What great thighs he has; I wonder if he's a biker.)

MICHAEL: Yes, it must be from Dean and DeLuca's. (What broad shoulders she has; I wonder if she's a swimmer.)

JENNIFER: I don't get to Dean and DeLuca's often since I live at 79th and Third. (I might as well find out right away. If he lives in the Village, forget it, too inconvenient.)

MICHAEL: Really? I live at 78th and Lex, right near the Rosedale Fish Market. (Fabulous, if I stay at her place during the week, I can pick up my shirts at the Chinese laundry before I go to the office.)

JENNIFER: They have the best tortellini salad in town. Do you like the neighborhood? (I wonder if he runs around the reservoir.)

MICHAEL: Yes, I like it because I can run around the reservoir. (I wonder if she runs around the reservoir.)

JENNIFER: Same here. But it's a long trip down to Wall Street. (I wonder how many laps around the reservoir he does.)

MICHAEL: Oh, do you work downtown also?

JENNIFER: I'm at Salomon Brothers. Where are you? (Great, I can ask him to lunch.)

MICHAEL: I'm in the corporate department at Cadwalader, Wickersham and Taft.(If she's at Salomon Brothers, she probably works 8 to 6 and can pick up the kids at the day-care center).

JENNIFER: Let's have lunch. Here's my card. (If he's at Cadwalader, he probably works from 10 to 8 and can drop the kids off at the day-care center.)

MICHAEL: Here's my card. (Her card says that she's a vice-president. I bet she makes six figures. I think I'm in love.)

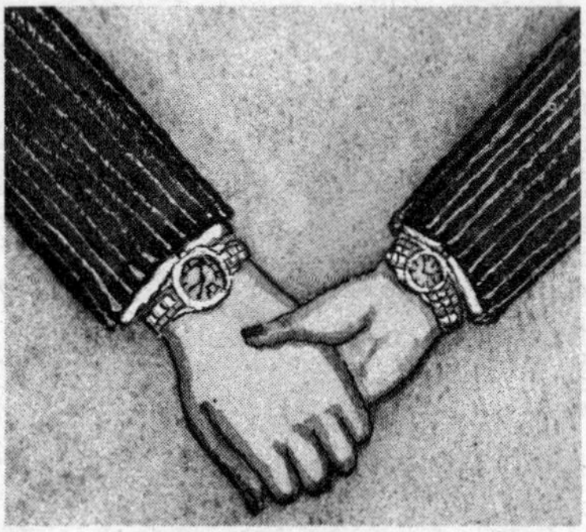

Does the Gold Rolex Yield More Satisfaction than the Big "O"?

Let's face it—sexually transmitted diseases have nothing to do with it. The real reason for the

New Celibacy is that Yuppies simply don't have time for sex. And a Yuppie would be the first to admit it. The only alternative to celibacy seems to be monogamy. Yuppie couples realize that occasional lovemaking is as necessary to their well-being as a brisk game of squash. But it takes careful planning to find time for personal activities in two hectic schedules already filled with therapy sessions, health club workouts, extended office hours and meetings of the co-op board. Take Michael and Jennifer, for example. Their evenings are so filled with outside commitments, they barely have time (or energy) for a good-night kiss at the end of the day.

Ironically, the less time Yuppies have to practice sex, the more they like to read about it. The well-versed Yuppie must not only be familiar with the state of the art in home computers, but also the latest in erogenous zones, G spots and exotic positions. You never know when the topic might come up at a dinner party. Yuppies also engage in sex as a pretext to play with their newest set of technological equipment. The Betamax, video camera, jacuzzi and hot tub are among the Yuppie's favorite sexual paraphernalia. ■

Don't's

1. **DON'T** enter new names in your address book unless you use pencil.

2. **DON'T** start knitting anything larger than a sweatband unless you're sure you can finish it before you break up (big needles help).

3. **DON'T** be afraid to ask about contagious diseases. Having herpes is even worse than having a half-finished sweater in the closet.

4. **DON'T** give up your apartment if you're moving in. By all means, sublet it on a day-to-day basis if possible. Even one weekend at your mother's can be unbearable when you've just divided up the kitchen equipment (especially if he keeps the ice cream maker).

5. **DON'T** ever have an affair with your boss. Falling out of love in this case usually means falling off the fast track.

6. **DON'T** consider celibacy an embarrassment. It's now a full-fledged movement; you can actually brag about it.

31. The Yuppie Wedding

Assuming the essentials are there and it's time to tie the knot, a Yuppie wedding is in order.

Here's what Yuppie weddings have:

Champagne
Poached salmon
A string quartet
A double-ring ceremony
A double-chaplain ceremony
(if the couple is intermarrying)

Here's what Yuppie weddings don't have:

An accordion player
A cash bar
Little hot dogs in blankets
Bridesmaids dressed in sherbet colors
A schedule that permits a honeymoon

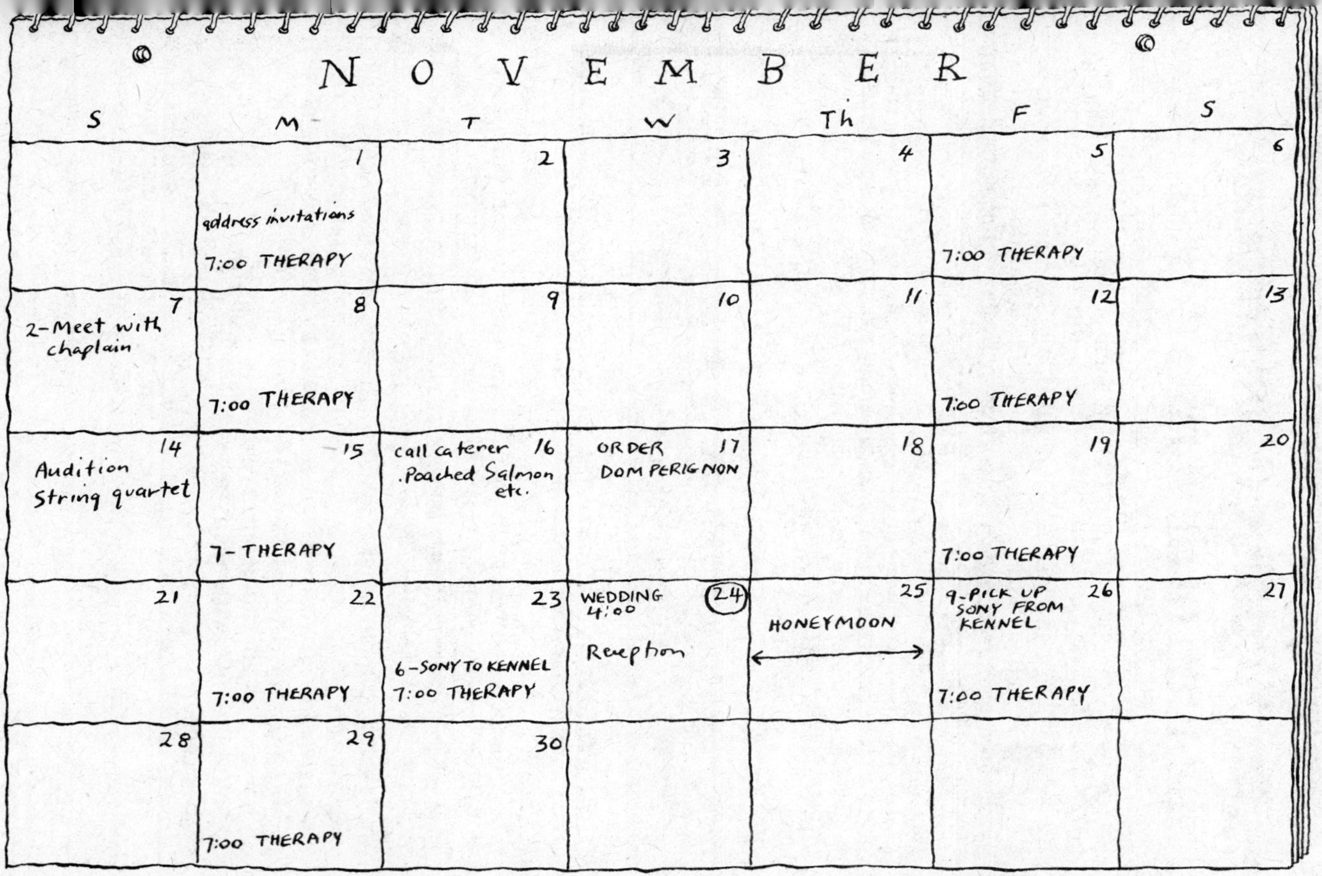
NOVEMBER
S M T W Th F S
1 address invitations 7:00 THERAPY
2
3
4
5 7:00 THERAPY
6
7 2-Meet with chaplain
8 7:00 THERAPY
9
10
11
12 7:00 THERAPY
13
14 Audition String quartet
15 7- THERAPY
16 call caterer .Poached Salmon etc.
17 ORDER DOM PERIGNON
18
19 7:00 THERAPY
20
21
22 7:00 THERAPY
23 6-SONY TO KENNEL 7:00 THERAPY
24 WEDDING 4:00 Reception
25 HONEYMOON
26 9-PICK UP SONY FROM KENNEL 7:00 THERAPY
27
28
29 7:00 THERAPY
30

32. Wedding Gifts: Software Instead of Silverware

THE BETROTHED Yuppie couple is likely to have acquired, even before their wedding, a full line of decorative and kitchen accessories. What do you buy as a wedding gift for two people who already have the 15-piece Le Creuset enameled cookware set in caviar grey and enough Waterford to open a branch of Tiffany's? Besides, a lovely little Lenox swan won't thrill a 32-year-old corporate vice-president the way it will a 20-year-old graduate of Briarcliff Junior College.

To achieve effective wedding gift-giving, one must do thorough research and exercise creativity and imagination.

Here are some suggested approaches:

Flora and Fauna: Add to existing collections or create a new category.

Examples: Saltwater tropical fish, orchids in bloom or a parrot trained to speak a phrase meaningful to the bride and groom

Hobbies: Supplies make good gifts.

Examples: A year's supply of wax to go with their cross-country skis or an entire ounce of saffron to go with their new paella pan

Lessons/Classes: Try something new.

Examples: Technical rock climbing, hot-air ballooning, condominium pricing

Subscriptions: Renewals are safest.

Examples: Health club, ballet or repertory theater (stay away from five free sessions at the couples' therapist)

Software: Writing a special program for the couple's home computer is today's equivalent of yesteryear's homemade quilt. ■

33. From Yuppie to Puppie

AFTER THE HAPPY couple has spent a few months integrating their possessions, using their new pasta machine and carpeting the platforms in the loft, it might be time to think about the replication of the species. Before any IUDs are removed or diaphragms thrown out, however, the following checklist should be completed:

- Has the condominium purchase agreement been executed and financing obtained?
- Has disability insurance been purchased, if necessary?
- Has the prospective mother already been made a partner or vice-president, whichever is applicable?
- Have all dissertations been completed? (There's nothing worse than a mother or father with an A.B.D. degree—All But Dissertation—trying to compile data with an infant wailing in the next room.)
- Has indoor plumbing been installed in the country house?
- Has the Mercedes 380 SL been traded in for a Volvo station wagon with a kiddie seat in the back?
- Has a videotape featuring an exercise program for pregnant women been purchased? (There's a good chance you'll have to give up your 7:00 A.M. aerobics class due to morning sickness.)
- Have you told your cleaning person that you won't be able to change the cat litter from now on, because of the danger of toxoplasmosis?

If the answer is yes to all of the above, consider yourself ready.

When a Yuppie couple decides it's time to reproduce, they set out to accomplish the task with the same obsessive efficiency they apply to everything else in life. The aspiring mother usually goes into training several months before the diaphragm is actually relegated to its plastic clamshell for good. Her high-protein, low-fat diet resembles that of a top-flight athlete. Nutritional supplements replace *haute cuisine* sauces, and even white wine is completely banished. She will pad her exercise program with extra aerobics and workouts for the abdominal muscles.

The couple will probably want

to try to control the sex of the child, thereby necessitating menstrual cycle tracking and basal thermometer charts even before any possible fertility problem may appear. (The secret to sex selection is impregnation early in the cycle for a girl, later for a boy.)

If the candidate for motherhood hasn't conceived by the second or third month, the Yuppie couple is sure to launch a full-scale fertility campaign involving counselors, physical examinations, sperm counts and dietary adjustments. After all, many Yuppie pregnancies require careful long-term as well as short-term planning. If conception takes too many months, will the delivery conflict with a national ad campaign the mother has planned for one of her accounts?

Once successfully impregnated, there's so much for the gleeful Puppie to do:

- The shopping is endless. After assembling the proper wardrobe (business suits, leotards, running shorts and even leather pants now come in maternity sizes), the nursery must be equipped with stacks of flashcards, a high-tech Aprica stroller and scores of other items that will guarantee the Yuppie baby a toehold on the fast track.
- Lamaze classes and pediatrician interviews are time consuming, as are field visits to potential birthing facilities and weekly meetings of the Financial Women Vice-President's Prenatal Club.
- A lot of creative energy must go into proper prenatal nutritional planning. Since sugar, alcohol and caffeine are all no no's, a Puppie must be clever enough to find something other than red wine to poach her pears in. Scrutiny for chemical additives must be stricter than ever, and important questions such as to B_6 or not to B_6 must be answered.
- Through it all, a Puppie will inevitably manage to wax eloquently and endlessly about prenatal exercise, what music to play for the fetus, the benefits of *in utero* massage and the emerging role of the Yuppie father.
- Speaking of which, Dad must be fully informed on all of the above and exhibit at least a few sympathetic pregnancy symptoms. ■

34. The Joy of Fathering

WHEN THE BIG day arrives and the contractions are coming every five minutes, the Yuppie father will arrive at the hospital with his panting wife in tow, usually lugging some form of photographic equipment to record this major event. At the very least, a Polaroid, but for really ambitious Yuppies, a video camera is more like it. In between ordering his Puppie to pant-blow and take deep cleansing breaths, he'll be busy photographing the arrival of his new offspring.

Should a Cesarean be necessary because the baby is so big and healthy, both Yuppie parents will be terribly disappointed and might even go so far as to try for a second child.

As soon as baby is born, a true Yuppie mother will clap him to her breast for infant bonding purposes, and while this will pay big dividends in the future, Dad should get in there and try to make his presence felt as much as possible. Unfortunately for him, he can't really compete with a built-in bottle. Yuppie fathers are best advised to adopt a future-oriented attitude. After all, how long can breast-feeding last? Only a few months at most, as Yuppie mothers are loath to extend their maternity leaves. And even if the Yuppie mom is a real showoff who dashes home on her lunch hour to continue breast-feeding after she's back at work, bottle-feeding is sure to creep in eventually.

In fact, really thoughtful Yuppie mothers introduce the breast pump almost immediately so Dad can have a chance to get up in the middle of the night and feed the little darling too (with a pre-filled bottle of Mother's milk). Dad may also bear chief responsibility for bathing baby or taking him to the doctor.

Which brings up another rough spot for the Yuppie father: how to explain child-related absences to the boss. (Remember Dustin?) It's safest to say you have to see the doctor yourself. Leave the kid out of it.

If parenthood gets a bit overwhelming, cheer yourself up with the reminder that it offers ever-increasing opportunities for one of a Yuppie's favorite pursuits—shopping. The kid will need a new wardrobe at least every two months. And then there are the education toys, Steiff stuffed animals, Lionel trains etc., etc. . . . ■

35. What Shall We Name the Baby Yuppie?

IN THE BEGINNING, there was Joshua. And Jason, Jonathan and Jonah. Then there was Benjamin, Daniel and Noah. All along there had been Rachel, Rebecca and Sarah. Most Yuppie nursery school rosters read like condensed versions of the Old Testament.

Then Woody Allen put Mia Farrow in a film and called her Ariel. It caught on like wildfire, but cautious Yuppie parents, envisioning classrooms filled with little Ariels, branched into other names that began with vowels. Popular today are Alexis, Alexandra, Allison, Amanda, Aaron, Eli, Emily, Ezra, Ethan, Evan and Ian.

Expectant parents are now more concerned with appropriateness. Are they giving their child a name the kid can live with? Get into graduate school with? Does it have too many letters to fit standardized test forms? How does it look on a mock-up of a business card? A memo pad? A nameplate?

Here's what Yuppies steer clear of:

- *Very ethnic names*. Being a Yuppie means being an investment banker who just happens to be Italian, not the other way around.

- *Very Preppie names*. Naming your kid something like Chatsworth Osborne, Jr. means you run the risk of having him end up breeding horses instead of going to business school.

- *Names that give clear career hints*. It's every Yuppie child's birthright to decide whether to go to law school or business school. And a banker named Clarence Darrow Schwartz makes everyone wonder if he couldn't get into law school.

NOTE: Unique spellings enable Yuppies to give more pedestrian names a certain flair. Fillice for Phyllis, for example. Consider also Noa, Iyan, Jasyn, Mykel, Kahnee, Muryelle and Alysin.

Unique spellings are not at all difficult to come up with. Just think phonetic—er, fenetic. ■

Predictions for the Future:

These names could be real comers.

Share—If you're into the stock market, generous divorce settlements or renting beach houses, this could have special significance. It has the added advantage of being totally androgynous.

Maris—Particularly apt if you like baseball.

Durry—Change the spelling and no one will know the kid's been named after a rug.

Adida—Who says your child can't remind you of your favorite sport?

Booth—Coming on strong with AT&T stockholders. (Add an "e" if it's a girl.)

Chauvan, Chauvanne—For boy/girl twins, a perfect choice, particularly if the mother is an avid feminist.

36. Kids On The Fast Track

0 years — Baby Yuppie is born one month early, which pleases her parents since this can mean an early school admission. The child is named Emily, which means "industrious."

8 months — Emily successfully completes her "Water Babies" swimming course and receives her minnow certificate.

1 year — Emily celebrates her first birthday at a pool party, with alumni of her swim course. Emily is clearly the best swimmer, but her parents are concerned because she hasn't yet spoken her first word. Fearful that she will grow up to be an inarticulate jock, they cancel her Tumbling for Tots course.

1 year 1 month — Emily speaks her first word. It is spoken in the kitchen at milk and cookie time. Emily's first word is "biscotti."

1 year 2 months — Emily enrolled in Tumbling for Tots.

2 years — Emily does an independent project for art class—a sculpture piece made from green, red and white pasta. She brings the project with her to her nursery school

interviews and is a big hit. Emily gains admission to the nursery school of her choice.

3 years Parents attend open school week and are told by Emily's teacher that her favorite activity is building high-rise condominiums with her Lego set. They promptly subscribe to both *Architectural Digest* and *Real Estate Weekly*.

4 years Emily takes her first ski vacation and shows great talent on the bunny slopes. She decides to buy her own skis and considers doing her undergraduate work at the University of Colorado. Her parents worriedly remind her that Cambridge is only a few hours from Vermont.

5 years Due to her late autumn birthday, Emily is able to begin first grade. After considering many offers, she decides on school in close proximity to an ice skating rink, evidencing a continuing commitment to winter sports.

6 years Emily attends day camp and is placed in the Wellesley group. Amanda, her best friend, is separated from her and put in the Radcliffe group. Furious, Emily refuses to attend camp. Her frantic parents debate whether this calls for a family therapy session. Emily also threatens to boycott the therapy session. The crisis blows over

when Emily and Amanda are both transferred into the Vassar group, which is more fun anyway, since it's co-ed.

7 years — Emily is chosen to dance in *The Nutcracker Suite* with the city ballet at Christmas. This means dropping both Chinese cooking class and figure skating lessons, but Emily decides that it is worth it.

8 years — Emily scores highest in her class on the standardized reading exam. She decides to buy only hardcovers from now on.

9 years — Emily switches schools due to inadequate computer facilities. She transfers to one that offers parent and child courses after school, since Emily feels fine about her own skills, but her parents lack a firm grasp of even the basics.

10 years — Emily is written up in a local magazine for an award-winning independent research project concerning the various parasites potentially contained in raw fish. Emily swears off sushi and spends the prize money on new skis, her own ice cream maker and a new wardrobe from the "Kamali for kids" section of Bloomingdale's.

11 years — Emily spends her spring vacation in Los Angeles, visiting a girl friend who used to be in her therapy group. Upon her return, she sells a magazine piece entitled "The Sociological Implications of Val Speak," so that her parents can write off the trip.

12 years — Emily signs up for a puberty-consciousness-raising course to help her make a smooth transition to the teenage years. Her parents at once register for the seminar, "Coping with Adolescent Aggravation." They recognize that Emily's years as a Yuppie child are over. ■

During the summers, Yuppie kids do not:

1. Work as a waitress or waiter at the Jersey shore. (Hiring on as an au pair on Nantucket or Cape Cod, however, is acceptable.)

2. Volunteer at a center for underprivileged children—unless the center is located in someplace interesting like India or Nicaragua.

3. Hang out at McDonald's or the mall.

4. Go camping in a recreational vehicle.

5. Visit Disneyworld, Disneyland or Epcot.

6. Stay home and watch TV.

37. Yuppie Divorce

ALIMONY IS FOR housewives and palimony is for rock stars. Lump-sum settlements are for Yuppies. Because it's assumed that both partners have decent salaries and hectic schedules, custody and child support are often split down the middle. All that's left to fight over is the condominium, the country house and the Akita. That's where the lump-sum settlement comes in—although many Yuppies feel that even the entire market value of the condominium won't compensate for the carefully chosen oak kitchen cabinets, the track lighting and the irreplaceable parking space.

Divorce is no stigma in Yuppie culture. On the contrary, Yuppies view their divorced status as a badge of an exalted state of consciousness that comes from having a vaster wealth of experience. "I'm divorced" is something Yuppies say with pride, the way they say "I've been to Egypt" or "I have my scuba diving certification."

Divorced Yuppies are a better prospect for a relationship. They understand mortgage financing and have a good idea of where the interest rates are going. Their kitchens are better equipped since they've undoubtedly negotiated for half the wedding gifts.

Prospective employers, formerly wary of the potential for instability, have come to regard divorced employees as good job candidates. They're responsible for child care only half the time and exhibit tendencies toward workaholism in order to get over their recent emotional trauma.

What leads to Yuppie divorce? There are basic incompatibility factors that can be spotted from the beginning—

- One partner insists on downhill skiing, while the other will only cross-country.
- One wants a country house in the mountains, while the other prefers the beach.
- One partner likes Szechuan while the other eats only Cantonese.
- Dovetailing schedules that seem great for child-care purposes can prove dangerous. When you find yourselves penciling each other in for breakfast, you know you're in trouble.
- Infidelity is not a widespread reason for Yuppie divorce. Most Yuppies don't have the free time to negotiate an affair or even a quickie dalliance. What is problematic is a Yuppie who

finally realizes after years of therapy that he or she is actually a Guppie. Or a Yuppie who only enjoys sex in the morning and has a spouse who refuses to give up his or her post-dawn squash game. (Weekday morning court time is not easy to come by.)

Divorce lawyers catering to Yuppies are catching on to the fact that it's a whole new ballgame out there. Other concepts they're boning up on are:

Prenatal agreements: Entered into before the birth of the child, they govern child support and custody provisions in case of divorce. They are also used by Yuppies who are too cautious, too independent or too busy to get married, but decide they want to replicate for business or personal reasons.

Apartment remodeling compensation: The Yuppie who must move out of the jointly held abode (usually the one who initiates the divorce proceedings) must be not only compensated for half the cost of renovations but also financially redressed for enduring the psychic pain of remodeling. Recognition must also be paid for the deprivation of that one-of-a-kind wall hanging and the Spanish bathroom tile that is now discontinued.

Joint possession custody: Rather than be separated from their cherished objects forever, Yuppies are now initiating programs where, although divorced, they share possessions of the carefully selected belongings. In other words, the Gelati ice cream maker goes to him one month, and her the next. He hangs the Robert Rauschenberg in his living room for half the year, while she places it in her foyer for the other half. After consultation with a pet psychiatrist, this concept has been successfully applied to all resident pets except cats, who are usually stubborn, inflexible and highly resistant to possession sharing. (They demand that the couple make a final choice.)

Visitation rights for the country home: Although one Yuppie usually buys out the other's share in the country home, an increasing trend is for the bought-out Yuppie to have privileges for one or two weekends a year.

Scheduling for restaurant dining: To avoid awkward encounters, Yuppies have their lawyers arrange who gets to go to the favorite Italian trattoria or French bistro on which night. Usually for the duration of one year, this prevents those sticky times when one freshly divorced Yuppie with a new beau meets her former spouse with his new girl friend. Some pioneers are expanding this concept to movie theaters and athletic clubs. ■

38. Stepparenting: Child-Raising by Proxy

PROS

1. For the Yuppie who feels full-time parenthood would interfere with a career, stepparenting can be a reasonable facsimile. The female Yuppie stepparent sidesteps pregnancy, maternity leaves and breast-feeding. Both male and female Yuppies can indulge in the art of parenting without full-time commitment. In most cases, the noise and mess will be a problem only every other weekend.

2. If a Yuppie wishes to have offspring of his own, the stepchild provides a perfect opportunity to judge the potential spouse's parenting abilities. Likewise, there's a ready-made print-out of the prospective mate's genetic material.

3. If the kid is a computer genius or media star, he might not only augment social standing, but also increase total annual income.

4. Like parenthood itself, stepparenthood offers endless new opportunities for shopping and buying.

5. If nothing else, the stepchild can provide a source of additional tax deductions.

CONS

1. It's hard enough to juggle two complex, high-powered schedules, let alone three. Will the Yuppie stepparent be able to keep up with family therapy, in addition to individual and couples counseling? Not to mention the occasional children's theater performance?

2. The ready-made child may have a ready-made pet with bad habits like ripping up Breuer chairs. Or the Yuppie stepparent may turn out to be allergic to the kid's Peruvian guinea pig. Even worse, the stepchild could be allergic to the Yuppie step-parent's *own* pet—especially that beautiful Abyssinian cat purchased for a three-figure sum.

3. The kid will surely have to have his own room or at least his own space in the apartment. Does this mean giving up plans for a media room? Or worse yet, purchasing an unsightly high-riser or convertible couch instead of a more stylish modular?

4. Tax deductions notwithstanding, private schools, summer camp and piano lessons are expensive. Will the kid's upkeep payments plunge the combined disposable incomes below acceptable standards? ■

COPING MECHANISMS

39. Psychotheryuppy

IT'S SEVEN P.M. on a Tuesday evening, prime time for Yuppie psychotherapy. The seven o'clock appointment is the most desirable and sought after—some Yuppies spend years with their therapist before they achieve a seven o'clock slot. (A six o'clock slot means you have a job with little responsibility, and an eight o'clock is awkward: it necessitates either eating before therapy or spending the entire session thinking about food—and all self-respecting Yuppies know that dinner before eight o'clock is only eaten by people who use bottled salad dressing.) An alternative to the seven o'clock appointment is the eight A.M. appointment. This serves a dual purpose: it frees up an additional evening for the gym and makes the statement that you have enough status in the office to come in late on a regular basis.

Anyway, it's seven P.M. on a Tuesday evening. The Yuppie enters the therapist's office and seats himself in a stressless chair. The session begins . . .

YUPPIE: I've had a very rough week. I decided that I'm not interested in having a relationship with Ellen, after all.

THERAPIST: Let's explore this issue a bit. Last week you were having feelings of ambivalence, but now you seem quite definite. What led to this decision?

YUPPIE: Ellen knows I have excellent subscription seats to the ballet, so when I invited her last week, she was delighted to accept. I was looking forward to it and even left work early to go to the gym and take a sauna before curtain time. We met in the theater lobby and she looked wonderful. Actually, she admitted to me that she had just come from the sauna too. There was something magical about the performance and about the evening.

THERAPIST: What happened after the ballet?

YUPPIE: It was a lovely night, and we decided to take a walk before dinner. We talked about intimate things and I felt very close to her. The feeling lasted through dinner. We went to a restaurant with a breathtaking view. We were in such a festive mood that we ordered champagne, which made the lights below us seem to twinkle even more. The food was excellent and she invited me to her apartment for dessert.

THERAPIST: Did you feel any anxiety about the thought of going home with her?

YUPPIE: Absolutely not. We had been out together several times and I felt that the time for sexual intimacy had arrived. I kissed her in the elevator and the prospects seemed promising. We went into the kitchen and she started to make coffee. And then *it* happened.

THERAPIST: What happened?

YUPPIE: She pulled out a jar of instant coffee. I was horrified. This is a woman with an MBA, who makes fifty thousand a year, who owns a condominium that must have cost at least one hundred thou, who wears a gold Rolex watch and knows enough about ballet to write a treatise. How could she use instant coffee? She didn't even offer an explanation. All she said was "Milk?" as she dissolved those dessicated crystals into boiling water and handed me the cup. I was so taken aback I couldn't even answer. I just took the vile substance and sat down on the couch. Of course, I didn't drink it.

THERAPIST: Were there any other events that contributed to your feelings of alienation from Ellen?

YUPPIE: Truthfully, I was so

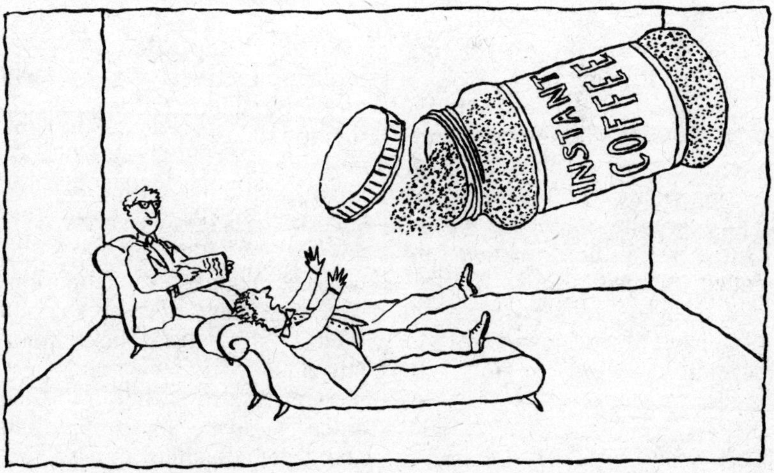

turned off at that point that I didn't even want to discuss it. I feigned a severe headache, made some vague reference to getting together again and fled.
THERAPIST: Now that you've had a few days to think about it, what are your thoughts about the incident?
YUPPIE: Frankly, I think that if I'm going to work on getting over my fear of intimacy, it's going to have to be with a woman who grinds her own beans.

At some point in a Yuppie's life, he or she will probably decide to enter therapy. The decision might come on the heels of a crisis, such as getting a divorce or being turned down for the vice-presidency of a division. Or the Yuppie might simply be envious of other Yuppies who discuss their psyches with Freudian insight, almost as if they were discussing a Bergman film.

Yuppies choose a therapist with the same serious deliberation that they display when selecting home video equipment. The search undoubtedly will include many field inspections called "consultations." Before embarking upon a costly series of consultations, however, three threshold decisions must be made:

1. What type of therapy is needed? Individual, couple, group or any combination of the above.

2. What school of therapy would be most helpful? Is there enough time for traditional four-morning-a-week analysis, or does a demanding schedule call for short-term goal-oriented behavior modification?

3. Is theme therapy appropriate? If so, what's the theme?

Theme therapy is the psychological equivalent of spot reducing. It's for those "problem areas" that create stumbling blocks in a Yuppie's eternal striving for perfection. The same themes recur throughout Yuppie culture, resulting in well-established modes of theme therapy. These include:

Stress Adaptation: This is probably the most popular form of Yuppie theme therapy. Stress therapy focuses on such areas as megavitamins, bioenergetics, nutritional counseling and all sorts of massage. (See body therapy, p. 112.) But then stress is a favorite Yuppie preoccupation. The only thing more prestigious than talking about how much stress you're under is telling people about stress therapy. Also since Yuppies are ambivalent about relinquishing stress, successful terminations are rare.

Assertiveness Training: Favored by women who have just made their first court appearance and are eager to avoid further encounters that make them feel like a Christian meeting the lion. If the therapy is successful, their personalities will deteriorate to the point of resembling those of their colleagues.

Sex Therapy: Originated in the days when impotency and frigidity were still considered problems. These syndromes have been replaced by the disorder of the decade—asexuality. For many Yuppies, overworked and time-pressured from nursery school on, celibacy has become a way of life.

Intimacy and Commitment Training: If a program of sex therapy is successful, a follow-up course of intimacy training will probably be in order. Successfully treated female patients have even been known, in rare cases, to assume their husbands' surnames.

Ethnic Awareness Therapy: For Yuppies who have been over-assimilated, groups are formed to get them back in touch with their ethnic roots. Issues discussed include: "Why Italian Yuppie Women always marry Jewish Men," "The Nose Job and Its Psychosocial Implications," and "Why Bob Dylan Changed His Name from Bob Zimmerman." The session often ends with group chanting, such as "I am a Jew," "I am a Greek," etc.

Couples Therapy: Not really theme therapy per se, but certain themes are pervasive. In addition to commitment phobias, tracking problems are often discussed. Problems are intense when one partner is on a faster track than another, something that never occurred to husbands of yesteryear who expected only their mistresses to be fast. ■

40. Body Therapy

PSYCHOTHERAPY may be fine in the long run, but it won't necessarily cure the excruciating back and stomach pains that are the inevitable outcome of a high-stress Yuppie existence.

Shiatsu massage: A sort of acupuncture without needles, Shiatsu massage focuses on any of the 6,000 pressure points on a Yuppie body. Many Yuppies spend an evening a week balancing their energy this way.

Rolfing: This method of deep muscle massage embodies the Yuppie credo: no pain, no gain.

Reflexology: A popular form of foot massage. Yuppies often take courses so that they can perform this on each other.

Foot rehabilitation centers: These are springing up in all parts of town. Poshly furnished in museum-grade leather, these places cater to the incapacitated Yuppie whose life has been ruined by a jogging injury.

Chiropractors: Yuppies with bad backs or pains of dubious origin will have their spines aligned by a chiropractor. In this case, the lack of a medical degree is not important.

Nutritional counseling: This therapy involves spending an inordinate amount of time diagnosing various types of nutritional allergies and deficiencies. It also provides rare instances when you will find Yuppies and suburban matrons sharing a couch in the waiting room.

Facials and body wraps: Used by Yuppie women and Guppies to eliminate every possible blemish and inch of cellulite. ■

SUSTENANCE

41. Chic Eats

YUPPIES HAVE elevated cooking to the status of the performing arts. Starting with *nouvelle* and culminating in the New American cuisine revolution, food and its preparation have become a major preoccupation for even the most casual Yuppie. Culinary artistry now ranks with venture capitalism and sports medicine as an acceptable Yuppie occupation. Celebrity chefs include Alice Waters of Chez Panisse in Berkeley, Wolfgang Puck of Spago's in L.A., Lawrence Forgione formerly of The River Cafe and now of An American Place in New York and Paul Prudhomme of K-Paul's in New Orleans. Food critics such as Mimi Sheraton and Gael Greene and serious periodicals like *Gourmet Magazine* help the Yuppie stay abreast of what's in and who's out.

Yuppie food, be it *nouvelle,* New American, northern Italian or French peasant, is uniquely suited to the Yuppie lifestyle. Here's why:

Nutrition: Most Yuppies came of age in the late sixties and early seventies. Terms such as complete protein and cold-pressed oil were incorporated into their vocabularies at an impressionable age. Although they may serve wild rice instead of brown rice these days, they haven't forgotten that white sugar is a hard drug. Hence the emphasis on fresh, seasonal, wild, nonprocessed and organic ingredients. Can the cans.

In addition, most Yuppies try not to defeat the work of their cardiovascular exercises with heavy cholesterol-laden or cellulite-producing dishes. This explains the need for smaller portions, light sauces and vegetables stir-fried with polyunsaturated fats.

Finally the Wholeness movement—whole earth, whole food, whole wheat—gave rise to a tendency toward simplicity and integrity of ingredients. Seasonings shouldn't be submerged in a murky Wagnerian brew. Instead, they should be separate and intact—something that can be identified right off the top of the palate and discussed at length.

Time: Another reason for the simplicity factor. The *nouvelle* chef who has to create a new menu every day doesn't have a chance to spend all week preparing the sauce. For the amateur chef, time is even more scarce. Between late nights at the office and workouts at the gym, there isn't much time to simmer the now-disdained stew.

Technology: Add the Yuppie's time crunch to his love of technology and you have the makings of a kitchen equipment orgy. Professionals set a killing pace, glorifying the food processor, then resurrecting the blender after having relegated it to the dust bin. Even for home use, gadgets must be heavy-duty industrial strength.

Diversity: Yuppies are city slickers, choosing to live in urban areas because of the cultural diversity. They also revel in exotica—that's why they go to Easter Island and Machu Picchu for their vacations. The outcome has been a penchant for anything foreign, especially the more obscure cuisines such as Ethiopian, Serbo-Croatian and Outer Mongolian. The same curiosity, paradoxically, has prompted Yuppies to dig up native roots—producing such discoveries as Jerusalem artichokes and fresh hearts of palm.

Appearance: Most likely it was the Japanese influence that spawned the current passion for presentation. A dish has to look right on the plate or it might as well be canned dog food. That means carved raw vegetables, fresh sprigs of mint and the right balance of color and shape. ■

42. Field and Stream: A Guide to Yuppie Ingredients

Veggies: In the salad department, avoid iceberg lettuce like the plague. Arugula and radicchio or wild chicory are the chic greens. Use them fresh or wilted under grilled fowl or baked cheeses. Romaine, watercress (especially wild), dandelion greens or anything hard to find in suburban shopping centers is fine.

Additional *au courant* vegetable matter includes truffles, wild mushrooms (chanterelle, morel, porcini and shitake), fiddlehead ferns, Jerusalem artichokes, fennel root and greens, wild day lilies (for salads and soups), turnips (very ethnic), leeks, red bell peppers and red chard.

Another noticeable trend is the Yuppie obsession with young vegetables: "new" potatoes the size of golf balls, "baby" corn the size of a pinky, "young" asparagus the size of a pencil. Cookbooks and gourmet magazines dwell on the tender age of produce in an embarrassing manner, especially in their color photography captions. This going on and on about tender, young succulent vegetables comes dangerously close to child vegetable pornography and, in our opinion, should be nipped in the bud.

Marine life: Fresh-off-the-boat and down-home varieties are best. That includes swordfish, catfish, periwinkles, conch, fresh tuna, salmon, crawfish, trout and American caviar. Anything made into sushi will pass.

Fowl: Along with fish, very Yuppie. Game birds of all kinds are at the top of the list—quail, partridge, pigeon, squab, etc. Duck is next. Chicken is suspect, unless you stick to the deboned breast.

Complex carbohydrates: Fresh pasta, new potatoes, and soba noodles are standard. Southern corn—grits, hominy, hushpuppies—is the rising star. Keep an eye out for Mexican versions of the native American staple. Homemade tortillas, perhaps.

Cheese: Going to the gourmet take-out store and picking a cheese has become as complicated a ritual as wine tasting: a sample of this or that, a cracker to clear the palate, a few cryptic comments about the age or region of origin, even a slight squeeze to test the ripeness. Yuppies like chèvre (or goat cheese) in imported and domestic varieties. We're not talking about feta from the deli here. Tortas from Italy (layered cheeses seasoned with herbs, mushrooms, fruits or nuts) are fashionable if you choose the right filling; basil torta is sure-fire Yuppie. Smoked or baked versions of old favorites (brie, mozzarella) give them sex appeal. Serve cheese as a separate course before or after the meal.

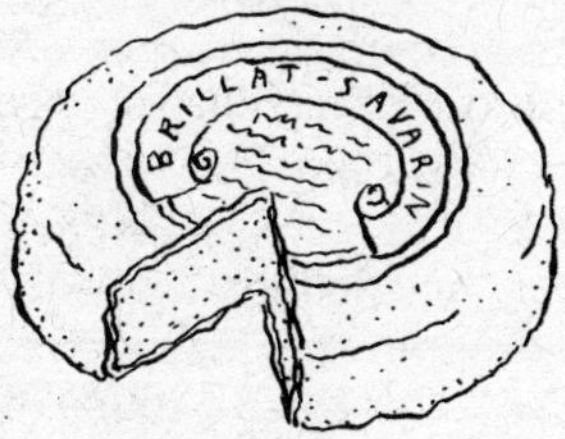

Meat: Many Yuppies have an aversion to red meat and won't allow it in their kitchens. If they get an uncontrollable urge, the usual remedy is a visit to the best-known local rib house for a platter of barbecue and a pitcher of Lone Star beer.

Condiments: Fresh herbs are *de rigueur.* Coriander is especially stylish. Try filé—a Cajun and Creole spice—red chilis and any of the fruits mentioned below—especially the berries—as sea-

soning. Wine will never go out of style as a condiment but try unexpected combinations like chianti with shellfish. Spirits such as vodka (throw some on your penne) and whiskey are catching on as well.

Yuppies do eat out a lot, but no matter how empty the refrigerator may be, a Yuppie pantry will *always* contain:

multiple vinegars (red wine, tarragon, raspberry, green peppercorn)
multiple oils (olive, walnut, hazelnut and sesame—with and without chili)
multiple mustards (smooth Dijon, grainy Dijon, English and German)
multiple coffee bean blends (French roast, Jamaican blue, espresso and water-processed decaffeinated)

multicolor peppercorns—black, white, green and pink (pink peppercorns are actually a type of berry that may cause an allergic reaction; pink peppercorn poisoning is a common Yuppie affliction)

Fruits: Wild berries (especially juniper, huckleberry, elderberry and blueberry), kiwi, beach plums, rhubarb and exotica of all kinds. Poach fruit in wine or marinate it in liqueurs for dessert.

Better still, make it into homemade ice cream or sherbet. If you don't have an ice cream maker (shame on you), buy a Yuppie brand and garnish it with a Yuppie topping like Scotch and a few grains of espresso coffee, freshly ground. NOTE: A commercial ice cream may be classified as Yuppie if it meets the following criteria: 1) its name must consist of two words, both foreign and unpronounceable; and 2) it must be expensive, e.g., Häagen-Dazs, Frusen Glädjé, Alpen Zauber. Häagen-Dazs is the original, of course. Legend has it that it was invented by a young entrepreneur who had inherited his parents' failing Bronx ice company. One morning he found a rubber stamp with a Danish map on it in the garbage, made up two Danish-sounding words and Yuppie ice cream was born.

Some final guidelines on what ingredients are Yuppie:

- Anything ethnic, especially regional American
- Anything that grew wild, especially if you had to gather it yourself
- Anything fresh, especially organically grown
- Anything smoked, except eels
- Anything imported, except from Taiwan
- Anything grilled over mesquite, fresh pine needles or hickory chips, except hot dogs ■

43. A Wine Primer: Are the Legs as Good as Betty Grable's?

BUYING AND ordering wine can be likened to investing in stocks and bonds. Unless you know what you're doing, make cautious and conservative commitments. Discreetly seek the advice of experts whenever possible. Learn the jargon, which can always get you by, no matter how limited your basic wine knowledge.

The most telling—and easiest to master—aspect of wine etiquette is ordering it in a restaurant. This should be handled with all the care and sensitive savvy that would be required in a major diplomatic mission.

Even if you know absolutely nothing about wine, you can make your way through tasting it without having to shrug apologetically. The following steps, taken dramatically yet in an understated manner, should result in pure theater.

When the wine steward brings the bottle, examine the label, memorize it for later use, nod and say "Very good." This is the only time you'll be able to say "Very good" without going out on a limb. All you're actually doing is complimenting the wine steward on his ability to read.

The wine steward will then decork the bottle and pour a little into your glass. If your wine steward is crass enough to offer you the cork to sniff (that's *his* job), just drop it in the ashtray. Cork-sniffing is one of the most glaring *faux pas* you can make, and anyone who tries to steer you in this direction deserves your utter disdain.

Hold the wine up to the light and look at its color. Murmur appreciatively "Very appropriate." Unless you're really up on subtle differences in shade, there's nothing else you can say. However, if the wine is completely opaque or has so much sediment in it that it looks like the Hudson River, action must be taken. In this case, look the steward sternly in the eye and say "That's inappropriate," just as a fourth-grade teacher or a psychotherapist might.

Swirl the wine in the glass. Do it slowly, because if you achieve more than 78 rpm, you'll end up staining your shirt. Examine the way the wine runs down the inside of the glass in lines. These are called "legs." You can say, "Look at those legs." It helps to think about Betty Grable while you're saying this, to lend emotional conviction. Examining the legs is a pointless preoccupation, but at least this way everyone knows that you're aware of their existence.

Hold the glass near your nose and take a few deep sniffs. Unless the wine smells rotten, smile and say with warm appreciation, "What a lovely bouquet." If you have difficulty mustering up warm appreciation, pretend that you're Leontyne Price on opening night. This lends the same emotional conviction that Betty Grable does to the legs, since to most people wine smells like wine.

Take a tiny sip and hold it in your mouth for a few seconds until the wine warms and the aroma rises into your nasal passages. Make subtle chewing motions to experience the full body of the wine. Swallow, pause a moment, looking upward, and then nod. Repeat the name of the wine (you should be able to do this without rechecking the bottle, which is why you were instructed to memorize the label at the outset). Nod to the steward with the merest hint of a smile. Grins and wide-mouth chuckles are obviously *outré*.

Congratulations, your ordeal is over. You have managed to taste the wine, making nothing but noncommittal statements and successfully hiding your complete ignorance. ■

DON'T'S

DON'T order rosé. Unless you can throw your weight around in the world of wine or are so rich it doesn't matter what kind of wine slob you are, this gaucherie is an opening for jokes back in the kitchen. It's okay, though, for picnics and cold buffets.

DON'T serve wine in the three-ounce goblets with hand-painted flowers that your grandmother gave you, unless the old girl is actually present.

DON'T drink hard liquor before good wine—it will spoil your palate—unless your boss is along and says, "Let's have a martini."

DON'T let the champagne breathe.

44. Useful Wine Words

Nouns

nose
bouquet
body
acidity
balance
texture
personality
intensity
nuance
style
complexity
character

Positive Adjectives

velvety
supple
lively
majestic
mature
concentrated
firm
tannic
charming
delicate
attractive
lovely
clean
bright
seductive
sturdy
robust
voluptuous
buttery

Negative Adjectives

pale
thin
acidic
anonymous
blurry
rough
dull
flabby
characterless
immature
closed
flat
harsh
overbearing

Words to Be Avoided in Describing Wine

good
tasty
fine
awful
stinko
yucky ■

FALLING OFF THE FAST TRACK

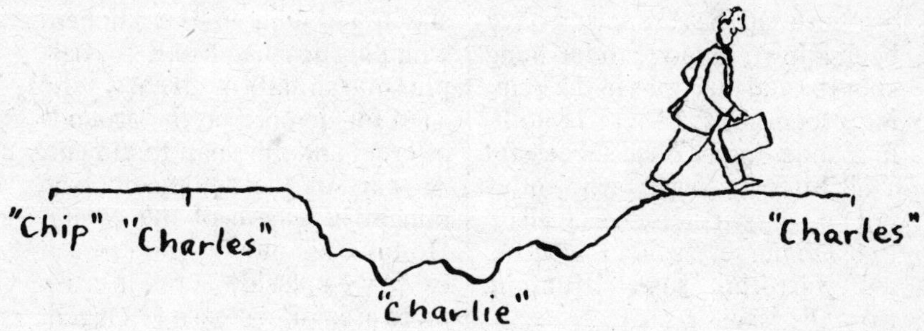

45. Yuppie Backlash: A Case Study

MOST YUPPIES manage to stay on the fast track, making at least twice their age in thousands per year. However, each year brings more victims of Yuppie burnout. Severe cases have been known to move to far-flung suburbs and take jobs in the helping professions. (There is nothing sadder than a once successful Wall Street attorney who, after not making partner, gives it all up to teach nursery school, wearing a T-shirt that says "Running from the Law.")

In Michael's case, the syndrome was triggered by a knee injury that kept him out of the gym for a month. During the first week, Michael thought he would not survive. He had that demented look that Yuppies get when they don't exercise for three straight days. The second week, however, he found that he enjoyed sitting in front of the television after work, nursing a six-pack. It brought back memories of his pre-Yuppie days and he soon forgot about the gym. Before he knew it, he found himself wearing sneakers instead of running shoes and playing Scrabble with his visiting mother. He developed a small paunch that he seemed almost fond of.

Jennifer was horrified. She looked the other way when he brought her dyed blue carnations on their anniversary, but when she found him in the kitchen, whipping up a batch of Rice Krispie marshmallow treats, she sued for divorce on the grounds of cruel and inhuman treatment. As part of the settlement, she bought his share of the condo. He took his money and spent it on forty lakeside acres in a remote area of northern Michigan. He fixed up the old cabin on the property and traded in his BMW for a half-ton pick-up. Jennifer

got the pasta machine and he bought himself an outdoor barbecue. Michael started a small woodworking business, a skill he had learned from his grandfather, who had been a carpenter in the old country, and settled happily into this peaceful existence until his Guppie brother Steven, a San Francisco architect, visited one summer. The brothers decided to completely redesign the cabin just for the fun of it. Michael's neighbor, a weekender who turned out to be the Home Design editor of a major Midwestern daily, was so impressed that she ran a feature on the renovation. Before they knew it, the brothers were flooded with requests for similar improvements. Steven decided to relocate to Michigan, having tired of endless Bay Area conversation about communicable diseases. They made plans to subdivide the 40 acres and build lakeside condominiums.

Marx Brothers Development Corp. is now worth eight figures, and Steven and Michael are active in five states. The moral: Once a Yuppie, always a Yuppie. ■

WHAT'S A REAL MAN'S BEST FRIEND? A REAL DOG!

Not to mention the other hilarious titles available to you from Pocket Books. You want fun? You got it! Ah, what the heck. Order all of 'em.

___44831 **REAL MEN DON'T EAT QUICHE** Bruce Feirstein $3.95
___46308 **REAL MEN DON'T COOK QUICHE** Scott Redman $3.95
___46309 **REAL WOMEN DON'T PUMP GAS** Joyce Jillson $3.95
___47757 **REAL DOGS DON'T EAT LEFTOVERS** Lee Lorenz $3.95
___46393 **AND THEN THERE WAS DUCK** John Ward $3.95
___49304 **RESTAURANT AT THE END OF THE UNIVERSE** Douglas Adams $3.50
___47709 **THE HITCHHIKER'S GUIDE TO THE GALAXY** Douglas Adams $3.50
___46726 **LIFE, THE UNIVERSE, AND EVERYTHING** Douglas Adams $3.50
___47394 **ROSEANNE ROSEANNADANNA'S "HEY, GET BACK TO WORK" BOOK** Gilda Radner with Alan Zweibel $4.95
___49892 **THE ROYAL BABY—THE PRIVATE LIFE OF HIS ROYAL HIGHNESS PRINCE WILLIAM,** a paper doll book $4.95
___49677 **THE COMPLETE AIR GUITAR HANDBOOK** John McKenna and Michael Moffitt $2.95
___47684 **THE YUPPIE HANDBOOK** Marissa Piesman and Marilee Hartley $4.95

POCKET BOOKS, Department LAF
1230 Avenue of the Americas, New York, N.Y. 10020

Please send me the books I have checked above. I am enclosing $________ (please add 75¢ to cover postage and handling for each order. N.Y.S. and N.Y.C. residents please add appropriate sales tax). Send check or money order—no cash or C.O.D.'s please. Allow up to six weeks for delivery. For purchases over $10.00, you may use VISA: card number, expiration date and customer signature must be included.

NAME ____________________

ADDRESS ____________________

CITY ____________________ STATE/ZIP ____________________ 807

☐ **Check here to receive your free Pocket Books order form.**

Home delivery from Pocket Books

Here's your opportunity to have fabulous bestsellers delivered right to you. Our free catalog is filled to the brim with the newest titles plus the finest in mysteries, science fiction, westerns, cookbooks, romances, biographies, health, psychology, humor—every subject under the sun. Order this today and a world of pleasure will arrive at your door.

POCKET BOOKS, Department ORD
1230 Avenue of the Americas, New York, N.Y. 10020

Please send me a free Pocket Books catalog for home delivery

NAME ______________________________

ADDRESS ______________________________

CITY ________________ STATE/ZIP __________

If you have friends who would like to order books at home, we'll send them a catalog too—

NAME ______________________________

ADDRESS ______________________________

CITY ________________ STATE/ZIP __________

NAME ______________________________

ADDRESS ______________________________

CITY ________________ STATE/ZIP __________

368